10/04

THE FATE OF THEIR COUNTRY

THE FATE OF THEIR COUNTRY

POLITICIANS,

SLAVERY EXTENSION,

AND THE COMING

OF

THE CIVIL WAR

MICHAEL F. HOLT

HILL AND WANG

A division of Farrar, Straus and Giroux

New York

Hill and Wang
A division of Farrar, Straus and Giroux
19 Union Square West, New York 10003

Distributed in Canada by Douglas & McIntyre Ltd.
Printed in the United States of America
First edition, 2004

Historical map of the United States courtesy of the author.
Map of Texas's contested boundaries copyright © 2004 by Jeffrey L. Ward.

Library of Congress Cataloging-in-Publication Data
Holt, Michael F. (Michael Fitzgibbon)
    The fate of their country : politicians, slavery extension, and the coming of the
Civil War / by Michael Holt.— 1st ed.
        p.   cm.
    Includes index.
    ISBN-13: 978-0-8090-9518-6
    ISBN-10: 0-8090-9518-1 (hc)
        1. United States—Politics and government—1845–1861.   2. United States—
History—Civil War, 1861–1865—Causes.   3. Political parties—United States—
19th century.   4. Slavery—United States—Extension to the territories.
5. Slavery—Political aspects—United States—History—19th century.   I. Title.

E415.7.H73   2004
973.7'11—dc22   2004040572

Designed by Abby Kagan

www.fsgbooks.com

1   3   5   7   9   10   8   6   4   2

In memory of William Gienapp

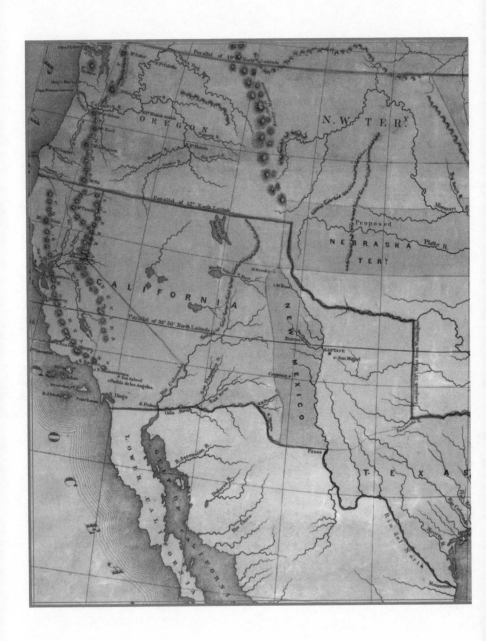

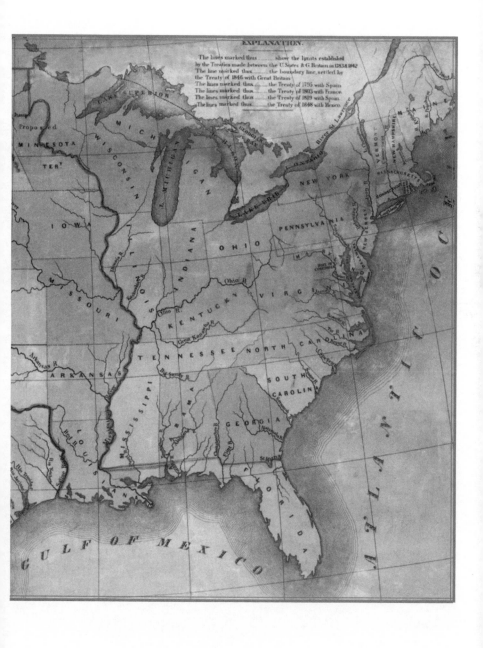

EXPLANATION.

The lines marked thus _____ show the limits established
by the Treaties made between the U. States & G. Britain in 1783 & 1842
The line marked thus _____ the boundary line, settled by
the Treaty of 1846 with Great Britain
The lines marked thus _____ the Treaty of 1795 with Spain
The lines marked thus _____ the Treaty of 1803 with France.
The lines marked thus _____ the Treaty of 1819 with Spain.
The lines marked thus _____ the Treaty of 1848 with Mexico

CONTENTS

This little book makes a simple yet vital point. What politicians do in elective office matters, often profoundly, to the lives of ordinary Americans. As I write in the spring of 2004, many of my fellow citizens would find this statement so obvious as to be banal. Relatives of soldiers stationed in harm's way know full well that any presidential administration can determine their loved ones' fate. Millions of Americans who have protested against the policies of George W. Bush's administration, impassioned fans of the candidates now vying for election come November, and residents of numerous states suffering the impact of budget cuts might all readily acknowledge the significance of elected politicians to their daily lives.

Nonetheless, the evidence of Americans' indifference to politics and to who is chosen to wield political power is overwhelming. Many Americans today cannot name their congressman or congresswoman, let alone their representatives in state legislatures. For almost forty years turnout rates of eligible voters in American elections have been scandalously low, especially among the young. Barely half of potential voters deign to participate in presidential elections, and estimates suggest that only 13 percent of those between eighteen and thirty years of age voted in the 2002 congressional elections. Meanwhile, among my fellow academic historians, many of whom have been the loudest in denouncing the current presidential administration's actions, American political history has become an object of scorn. Eager to celebrate the "agency" of those without formal governmental power, they denigrate the significance of past public policies, deny that everyday Americans paid serious attention to politics, and deride historical analysis of the actions of governmental officeholders as decidedly old hat, elitist, and inconsequential compared with more faddish interests in seemingly any group except the white male politicians who exercised formal political power in our past.

I believe that this dismissive view of political history is egregiously wrongheaded. It seriously underestimates the role of events beyond average citizens' personal control in affecting their lives and the crucial role that elected politicians often played in causing those events. One such transforming event, quite clearly, is war. It is evident as I write, for example, that the ongoing war in Iraq has already affected the lives of millions of ordinary Americans personally, as will its future economic and budgetary consequences affect hundreds of millions more. Academics are certainly ready to criticize the politicians who authored or allowed that war. If so, why are not the politicians who brought on the war against Mexico in the 1840s, the closest analogy in all of American history to the current war in Iraq, or the later Civil War equally worthy of scholarly scrutiny? No one can honestly argue that those nineteenth-century wars did not affect people's lives, from the families of soldiers who were killed to the southern slaves who seized the opportunity to escape to freedom during the Civil War.

To acknowledge war's undeniable impact is inevitably to raise the question of what caused it. And far more often than not, the preferred subjects of historians who today dismiss political history as passé did not in fact cause the wars that had such profound social, economic, and political consequences. To locate the most direct causes of the American Civil War, in which over 600,000 Americans died, for example, one must look at the actions of governmental officeholders in the decades before that horrific conflict. Their decisions and the impact of those decisions are the subjects of this book.

As much as I, like all historians, have been influenced by current events while writing, they are not the reasons I wrote this book. My former editor at Oxford University Press, Thomas LeBien, now publisher at Hill and Wang, asked me to do so. I initially resisted his entreaties. I had already written two longer books on this subject, and I had no inclination to recant the interpretations I advanced in them since I still believe they are correct. Thus I knew that I could say little that was new to my fellow historians who still care about the causes of the American Civil War. But this book is not aimed primarily at fellow experts or readers of my previous books. I have intentionally and with substantial effort kept it very short in order to reach a new and, I hope, wider audience.

As he did with my very long history of the American Whig Party, Thomas has provided expert editorial assistance in rounding this far briefer book into shape. To my joy, while I was drafting it, Professor William W. Freehling, the preeminent historian of the antebellum South's road toward secession, moved to Charlottesville, Virginia, where I live and teach. A true friend, he kindly, indeed eagerly, agreed to look at my scribblings. What a superb—and ruthless—editor! Line by line and sentence by sentence, he endeavored to make my lax prose more muscular. I have not always followed his injunctions. Nonetheless, I profoundly appreciate his help and especially his enthusiasm for the project itself. He, too, believes that in recent years our profession has unduly, and to its profound explanatory detriment, minimized the decisive importance of what political actors did in shaping the course of American history.

MICHAEL F. HOLT
Charlottesville, Virginia
March 2004

THE FATE OF THEIR COUNTRY

1

PANDORA'S BOX

In the winter of 1860–61, as one Deep South state after another seceded in a furious reaction to the November election of the Republican Abraham Lincoln as President, congressmen frantically sought to devise a compromise that would soothe southern tempers, lure seceded states back into the Union, and avert civil war. The compromisers aimed to reassure Southerners that the almost exclusively northern and now-victorious Republican Party represented no threat to slavery and what were called Southern Rights. So hoping, both the House and the Senate passed a proposed thirteenth amendment to the Constitution, with two-fifths of the Republicans in each chamber voting aye. This amendment would forever have prohibited the federal government from abolishing slavery. This action, so ironic in the context of what became the emancipating Thirteenth Amendment in 1865, hardly satisfied Southerners in 1861. Instead, they demanded that Republicans legalize the extension of slavery into all current and future western territories south of the parallel line thirty-six degrees thirty minutes. Congressional Republicans, pledged from the formation of their party in 1854 to bar slavery from all territories and urged by President-elect Lincoln to "hold firm, as with a chain of steel" against any compromise on slavery extension, refused to make that concession. Efforts at compromise collapsed. And the war came.

Thus attempts to resolve the secession crisis foundered on the question of slavery's future expansion into southwestern territories, where it did not exist, rather than on its guaranteed perpetuity in the southern states, where it already did. This phenomenon speaks volumes about the causes of the American Civil War. Most historians of the war's causation now agree that the issue that most aggravated sectional conflict during the fifteen years prior to 1861 was slavery's extension beyond the existing slave states, not demands for its abolition within them. That fact raises a host of questions. How and why did the issue of slavery extension emerge? Why did Northerners and Southerners apparently invest so much importance in that issue even when many believed that slavery could not exist profitably in most of the western areas they argued over so furiously? And why did this question prove so intractable? Like a bad weed, the issue popped up again and again after repeated attempts to yank it out had apparently succeeded. Raising the question of slavery's extension into or exclusion from the West truly was opening a Pandora's box of evils, for it could never again be closed. Why?

The slavery extension issue first emerged because of decisions by elected officeholders in the executive and especially the legislative branches of the national government in Washington, *not* because of a groundswell of public pressure for or against territorial and slavery expansion. The point is crucial. Sectional divisions widened in response to what politicians in Washington did; divergent sectional opinions about slavery and basic social and economic distinctions between the free-labor North and the slave-labor South did not in and of themselves cause those decisions. At few other times in American history did policy makers' decisions have such a profound—and calamitous—effect on the nation as they did in the 1840s and 1850s. Those decisions by themselves, it must be stressed, did not cause the Civil War. As Lincoln later said, that bloody conflict was "a people's contest," not simply a politicians' war. Rather, the decisions were crucial because they did so much to deepen distrust and intensify animosity between the white populations of the North and the South.

The slavery extension issue emerged in Congress in its most explosively divisive forms between 1846 and 1854. The issue, however, also arose on two earlier occasions in the nineteenth century with considerable impact on what happened later.

In early 1819, southern congressmen bitterly opposed a northern attempt to prevent Missouri's admission as a slave state. The ensuing debate was exceedingly rancorous, and it contained almost all the elements that would characterize sectional controversy over slavery expansion until the Civil War. Northerners condemned slavery as immoral, as economically inefficient, as incompatible with free labor, and as an undemocratic source of southern political power in the national government. They called Southerners already overrepresented in the House of Representatives and electoral college, thanks to the Constitution's three-fifths clause. If Missouri were admitted as a slave state, southern senators would gain a two-seat edge over Northerners. Southerners, in turn, furiously resented Northerners' critique of their "peculiar institution." More important, they worried that if Northerners in Congress could force Missourians to emancipate their slaves as the price of statehood, Northerners would use that precedent to seek the abolition of slavery in other slave states. That action would violate each state's sacro-sanct right to determine its own domestic institutions.

The congressional debate over Missouri, while rancorous, was also relatively brief compared with later quarrels over the Mexican Cession and Kansas. In March 1820, Congress passed the Missouri Compromise, even though most Northerners op-posed it. By this settlement, Congress admitted Maine as a free state to offset Missouri's admission as a slave state, thus preserv-ing the sectional equilibrium in the Senate. More important, Congress "forever prohibited" slavery in the unorganized area of the Louisiana Purchase territory north of the parallel thirty-six degrees thirty minutes. In the Senate, where all three provisions were bundled together in a single bill, only two of twenty-two Southerners opposed this package, despite its prohibition of slavery from the vast majority of the Louisiana Territory. In the House, where the ban on slavery north of what became famous as the Missouri Compromise line was voted on separately, all Northerners supported the prohibition while Southerners split narrowly 39–37 in its favor. In short, in 1820 a majority of southern congressmen accepted congressional prohibition of slavery from almost all of the western territories. The southern demand thirty-four years later that this prohibition be repealed in the Kansas-Nebraska Act was arguably the single most im-portant turning point on the road to disunion and civil war. That demand clearly reflected a shift in the southern position since 1820, and no action by Congress ever outraged the north-ern public so much as the repeal of the Missouri Compromise line.

The second incident involving slavery's westward extension before 1846 took a different form and had a more immediate impact on subsequent events. In April 1844, President John Tyler asked the Senate to ratify a treaty annexing the pro-slavery

Republic of Texas, which had won its independence from Mexico in 1836. Here the question was not prohibiting slavery from or allowing slavery into an area largely unoccupied by American citizens. It was whether to add to the Union an area where slavery was already legal, as had happened with the acquisition of Florida from Spain in 1819. More significant, the clash over Texas annexation took a decidedly partisan rather than sectional form. It did so largely because of a crucial intervening development between 1820 and 1844: the emergence of the nation's first truly mass-based two-party political system, a development that would critically affect all subsequent debates over slavery extension.

The Missouri crisis debates took a nakedly sectional form because, by 1820, the previous system of party competition between Federalists and Jeffersonian Republicans had collapsed and the Federalist Party had all but disappeared. Without an external foe to provoke internal party discipline and unity, Jeffersonians had fragmented along sectional lines over Missouri. In response, some exceptionally shrewd political leaders sought to revive interparty competition to preclude future sectional conflicts. Of these, New York's Martin Van Buren took the lead in constructing what became the Democratic Party behind Andrew Jackson's presidential candidacy in 1828. Called the "Little Magician" because of his political dexterity, Van Buren wrote a Virginia ally in 1827 that reviving a system of two-party competition between Jackson's friends and enemies would best neutralize "prejudices between the free & slaveholding states." "Party attachment," he declared, had once "furnished a complete antidote to sectional prejudices by producing counteracting feelings." The best way to restore that party loyalty was for northern and southern advocates of states' rights and strict construction to combine behind Jackson against incumbent President John Quincy Adams, whose broad construal of national power struck states' rights men as anathema.

Andrew Jackson's actions during his two terms as President between 1829 and 1837 went far toward reviving partisan attachments. To his avid supporters, Jackson's contempt for established social and economic elites, his determination to remove Indian tribes still east of the Mississippi River from their lands, and his war against the Bank of the United States made him seem a champion of the people against the privileged. His foes, however, regarded Jackson, or "Old Hickory," as his admirers called him, as a potential Caesar. His alleged dictatorial penchant for flouting Congress, the law, and the Constitution endangered the Republic. In 1834 these opponents began to combine under the banner of the new Whig Party. They chose the name to identify themselves with the Revolutionary patriots who had fought King George.

Initially, only common opposition to "King Andrew" held Whigs together, and they failed to prevent the election of Van Buren as Jackson's successor in 1836. Within months of Van Buren's inauguration in March 1837, however, a sharp financial panic occurred that quickly developed into a full-fledged depression. As a result, the battle between Democrats and Whigs moved from personalities to economic policies. Led by Van Buren, Democrats blamed the panic and depression on excessive paper money and rampant speculation. They called for the national and state governments to divorce themselves from the private economic sector. Any positive governmental economic action, they charged, inevitably produced inequalities, privileges for some at others' expense.

Whigs, in contrast, called for positive governmental action— the chartering of banks and other corporations, expansion of the paper-money supply and sources of credit, protective tariffs, and subsidies for the construction of roads, harbors, and canals (or internal improvements, as such developmental policies were then known)—in order to promote economic recovery and expansion. Riding this program, Whigs made stunning gains in the off-year gubernatorial, congressional, and state legislative elections between 1836 and 1840 as they attracted tens of thousands of new voters into the political process. In 1840 they swept the vast majority of those elections and won the presidency for the first time behind their ticket of "Tippecanoe and Tyler, Too." Over 80 percent of the nation's potential voters went to the polls, compared with only 57 percent in 1836. This huge voter turnout created a mass-based two-party system.

In the new system, Democrats and Whigs tried to mobilize their supporters by defining the differences between themselves as sharply as possible, whether over men or measures. In the American federal system, those differences defined state public policy as well as national policy. Because the sectional wings of the two parties supported a common candidate only once every four years, in presidential elections, Northerners and Southerners could usually take different positions from each other on slavery. Whigs and Democrats in, say, Pennsylvania or Mississippi could offer contrasting positions to their own voters without always agreeing with fellow party members from the other section. As a result, when politicians positioned themselves on issues, shortsighted calculations of partisan advantage often eclipsed any broad-minded concern about the Union. Such was the case with the introduction of the Texas issue into the national political arena—and with so many subsequent decisions involving slavery extension.

John Tyler, a slaveholding Virginian, had been elected Vice President on the Whig ticket in 1840. Tyler became President

when William Henry Harrison died a month after his inauguration as President. Tyler promptly vetoed some of the Whig
party's most cherished economic legislation. In response, Whig
congressmen and most state Whig organizations formally read
Tyler out of the Whig Party. Intent on redeeming his reputa-
tion, desirous of foiling his acerbic Whig antagonists, and
deeply devoted to the perpetuation of slavery, Tyler hit upon
the annexation of Texas as an issue on which he might win the
presidency in 1844. England's reported attempts to persuade authorities in the Republic of Texas to abolish slavery also influenced him.

Intransigently hostile to Tyler, Whigs in Congress and
around the country rallied behind the presidential candidacy of
their beloved leader Henry Clay. Clay had engineered the formation of the Whig Party in 1834, and he had galvanized congressional Whigs' opposition to Tyler. Two weeks before his
nomination in early May 1844, the Kentucky slaveholder Clay
wrote a public letter to southern Whig senators. He attacked
Tyler's intent to annex Texas as fraught with danger to the nation. Because Northerners objected to the addition of more
slave territory, let alone another slave state, he wrote, annexation
would inevitably erode the sectional comity on which the
Union was based. Just as important, Clay forecast that annexation would inevitably produce a war with Mexico, which had
never recognized Texas's independence. Opposition to Texas's
immediate annexation became the standard Whig campaign
theme in the presidential election of 1844, and in June 1844 all
Whig senators except two Southerners voted, successfully, to
reject Tyler's treaty of immediate annexation. Rallying around
Clay, the Whigs' standard-bearer in the presidential campaign,
reinforced the party's antagonism to Texas annexation. There-

after, politicos usually shaped policy in the extension debates that spiraled toward secession and war.

In 1844 most Whigs expected ex-President Martin Van Buren to be Clay's Democratic opponent in the presidential race. On April 27, the same day that Clay's anti-annexation letter appeared, Van Buren published his own anti-annexation letter in order to preserve his electability in the North. His closest northern Democratic allies in Congress had frantically warned him that "the Texas treaty is made upon a [pro-slavery] record that is sure to destroy any man from a free state who will go for it." Van Buren's stand, however, opened a chink in his political armor. Democratic opponents used his anti-annexation stance to block his nomination. At the Democratic convention they forced the adoption of a two-thirds rule that prevented Van Buren's simple majority of delegates from nominating him. Van Buren's opponents then secured the nomination of the pro-annexation Tennessee slaveholder James K. Polk and the adoption of a platform calling for "the reoccupation of Oregon and the reannexation of Texas at the earliest practicable period." Thus Democrats entered the campaign with a candidate and platform committed to immediate annexation.

Van Buren's disappointed followers loyally supported Polk's candidacy, but they raged that Texas annexation had been used to derail Van Buren's nomination. Thus when the Senate voted on ratification of Tyler's Texas treaty in June, eight Van Burenite Democrats, including Missouri's Thomas Hart Benton, New York's Silas Wright, and Connecticut's John M. Niles, joined all but two Whigs in the overwhelming majority that defeated ratification.

Tyler's treaty was dead. But the Texas annexation issue clearly helped Polk carry eight of thirteen slave states, thus contributing to his narrow victory over Clay in the November election. Polk also carried seven of the North's thirteen states, including the nation's two biggest electoral-vote prizes, New York and Pennsylvania. Nonetheless, with the possible exceptions of Illinois and Indiana, where the territorial expansion issue helped Democrats, northern Whigs had benefited enormously from Clay's opposition to the westward expansion of slavery. And since annexation also might result in war with Mexico, Van Buren prophetically warned his Democratic allies in Congress as early as February 1845 that "too much care cannot be taken to save us [northern Democrats] from a war" that northern Whigs "shall be able to charge with plausibility" that we Democrats wage "for the extension of slavery."

The Democrats' triumph in the 1844 elections increased the odds of Texas annexation, but it did not ensure it, since so many northern Democrats personally opposed slavery's extension and, for political reasons, feared flouting the dominant sentiment in the North against it. Yet Texas was annexed in 1845 and in a way that outraged most Whigs and many northern Democrats.

When the short second session of the Twenty-eighth Congress met in December 1844, lame-duck President Tyler immediately asked it to offer Texas annexation by passing a joint resolution that would require only a simple majority vote in the House and Senate. This tack would avoid the far-more-elusive two-thirds Senate majority required to ratify a treaty. With their heavy majority in the House, Democrats could easily pass the resolution containing the same terms as Tyler's rejected treaty. Aware of this near certainty and that their party had been damaged in the South by the annexation issue in 1844, a few southern Whigs were now eager to annex Texas. If annexation came now, they hoped, the issue would not hurt southern Whigs during the impending congressional and gubernatorial elections of

1845. Led by Tennessee's Milton Brown, moreover, they saw an opportunity to turn the annexation issue to their own partisan advantage; southern Whigs could be portrayed as even more ardent champions of slavery and the South than southern Democrats. As would happen so often in the future, slavery extension became a political weapon rival parties vied to exploit for political reasons.

Under the original terms of the Democratic resolution, Texas would be admitted to the Union as a territory, not as a state; furthermore, in return for paying off the bonded debt Texas had accrued since 1836, the United States would own all the unsold public land in the huge republic. According to Brown's amendment, Texas would retain its public lands but also its debt. His amendment also stated that the United States should take responsibility for settling the disputed boundary between Texas and Mexico, for Mexico continued to insist that the Nueces River, not the Rio Grande, formed the southern and western border of Texas just as it had when Texas was a Mexican state. More important, Texas would be admitted as a new slave state with voting privileges in Congress. What is more, Brown stipulated that as many as four additional states could be carved from Texas and that future Congresses must admit them as slave states if Texans so desired. In short, Brown's amendment could add as many as ten new slave state senators. Under the plan, exulted one Tennessee Whig congressman, "the South would acquire a wonderful increase in political power."

The House adopted Brown's amendment. But that form of annexation distressed many northern Democrats, to say nothing of northern Whigs and a surprising number of southern Whigs as well. In its amended form, the annexation resolution passed the House 120 to 98. The majority included 112 Democrats and only 8 southern Whigs. The minority was composed of 26 fu-

rious northern Democrats and 72 more furious Whigs, 17 of
whom represented slave states. Altogether 90 percent of the
Whigs opposed and 81 percent of the Democrats supported the
measure. The division over annexation remained more partisan
than sectional.

Because of this partisan alignment, Senate passage of the
Brown annexation proposal proved difficult. Whigs still held a
three-seat majority in the Senate, and most of the northern Democratic senators who had voted against Tyler's treaty found the
Brown amendment even more obnoxious. They denounced annexation as "wholly a struggle for political power at the South,"
pushed solely "for the benefit of the South; for the strengthen-
ing of her institutions, for the promotion of her power." As the
congressional session neared its mandated end in early March
1845, therefore, the annexation resolution seemed to be perish-
ing in the Senate.

It was saved by the very Van Burenite Democrats who abhorred the House bill. Missouri Democrat Thomas Hart Benton, renowned as "Old Bullion" Benton because of his rocklike
devotion to Jacksonian hard-money policies, successfully moved
an amendment that gave incoming President Polk two options.
Polk could offer Texas annexation under the terms of the House
bill, or he could negotiate new terms with Texas authorities.
Benton, an antislavery man from a border slave state, and northern Van Burenite Democrats clearly expected Polk to pursue the
second option. Then only the small, populated eastern fraction
of Texas would be admitted as a slave state. The huge remaining
area it claimed would be unorganized territory. Slavery might
yet be excluded from it. In brief, they hoped to reduce the
South's gain in political power from Texas annexation. They expected Polk to pursue this option because Polk explicitly prom-

ised Benton that he would do so. Only that promise brought northern Democrats on board.

As amended by Benton, the annexation resolution narrowly passed the Senate 27–25. All twenty-four Democrats and three southern Whigs voted aye. Twelve southern and thirteen northern Whigs shouted nay. When this revised version arrived back in the House for action, party lines grew even starker. Every single Democrat and one southern Whig passed it over the opposition of every other Whig who voted. Despite the obvious sectional connotation of extending slavery by annexing Texas, partisan loyalties still outweighed naked sectional allegiance. An apparent verification of Van Buren's prediction that "party attachment" could be a "complete antidote to sectional prejudices," this achievement would quickly evaporate.

On his final day in office the apostate Whig Tyler foiled Benton and northern Democrats. He dispatched a courier to Texas offering annexation under the Brown-amended version of the House bill. Rather than recall this courier, Polk broke his promise to the Van Burenites and endorsed Tyler's action. Furthermore, rather than seek new negotiations to settle the boundary dispute between Texas and Mexico, as even Brown's amendment had called for, he declared the Rio Grande the recognized boundary and announced that he would deploy American military and naval forces to defend it. Furious Van Burenite Democrats never forgave Polk for his duplicitous betrayal. But the deed was done. In July, Texas accepted the offer of annexation, and in December 1845 Congress admitted it as a new slave state.

Polk called the Rio Grande the boundary between Mexico and the United States partly because he lusted for the country's expansion across the North American continent. Nor was he content with pushing the nation's boundary westward to the

Rio Grande. He sought the Mexican province of California and its ports on the Pacific coast, from which Americans could carry on trade with Asia.

Polk first tried to buy California from Mexico, but Mexican authorities rebuffed his emissary. The frustrated Polk then decided to provoke a war. He fully expected to win easily and to seize California as indemnity for America's war expenses. To do this, he focused on the still-disputed area between the Nueces River and the Rio Grande. He ordered troops commanded by Zachary Taylor to move to the northeastern bank of the Rio Grande near the Gulf coast. In May 1846, after Mexican troops attacked Taylor's soldiers for invading what they believed was Mexican soil, Polk told Congress that war had begun by an act of Mexico. He insisted that Congress raise the men and supplies necessary to fight Mexico's alleged aggression.

Whigs had almost unanimously opposed Texas's annexation and had never accepted its grandiose claim to all land north and east of the Rio Grande. That area encompassed more than half the Mexican province of New Mexico, including the trading center Santa Fe. Whigs furiously denounced Polk's justification for war. Recalling the political obliteration of the Federalist Party after it had openly opposed the War of 1812, however, most of them voted for the men and supplies needed to fight it. Polk's war of aggression equally outraged Van Burenite Democrats. "I fear," wrote New York's Democratic senator John A. Dix, that "the Texas fraud is carried out to its consummation by a violation of every just consideration of national dignity, duty, and policy."

The "fraud" Dix referred to was Polk's double cross on the terms of Texas annexation. He also correctly implied that Polk alone was responsible for the war. While Whigs had predicted war would inevitably result from Texas annexation, it could have

been avoided had Polk not declared the Rio Grande the boundary between Texas and Mexico and then used that claim to provoke a war to seize California. This was his decision. He used his power as commander in chief to deploy troops to pursue his personal agenda. He did not seek the prior approval of Congress, and few if any Americans were dreaming about California, let alone clamoring for its seizure from Mexico, during the fifteen months between his inauguration and the attack on Taylor's troops. By completing Tyler's equally shortsighted initiative, Polk had pried open the lid on a Pandora's box. He had created Van Buren's nightmare, "a war" that Whigs could "charge with plausibility if not truth" that Democrats "waged for the extension of slavery."

2

THE WILMOT PROVISO

In early August 1846, Polk sent Congress special messages asking for an appropriation of $2 million to pay Mexico for "any cession of territory" Mexico might make to the United States under the terms of a peace treaty Polk hoped to negotiate that summer. He thus made clear what had been an open secret since his war message to Congress the preceding May: Polk went to war to extract land from Mexico. Polk himself was not interested in getting land for additional slavery extension. Other southern Democrats, however, clearly were, and from the war's start numerous Northerners charged that spreading slavery still farther westward was the war's purpose. Thus, when the House took up Polk's request on August 8, a New York Whig congressman immediately demanded that it "be so amended as to forever preclude the possibility of extending the limits of slavery."

As Van Buren had warned, however much northern Democrats personally disliked slavery and opposed its extension, they faced political immolation in northern elections if Whigs could portray them as supporting a pro-slavery war. Even before the debate opened on August 8, therefore, a group of northern Democratic congressmen had agreed that the first one of them to gain the floor during the upcoming House debate should amend Polk's request by barring slavery from any land acquired as a result of the war. The honor fell to a hitherto-obscure freshman Democrat from northern Pennsylvania named David Wilmot, and his proposed amendment forever after became famous as the Wilmot Proviso. It provided "that, as an express and fundamental condition to the acquisition of any territory from the Republic of Mexico . . . neither slavery nor involuntary servitude shall ever exist in any part of said territory, except for crime, whereof the party shall first be duly convicted."

Northerners, who outnumbered Southerners in the House 134 to 91, quickly adopted Wilmot's amendment. The amended appropriation bill then passed the House on a starkly sectional vote. Every Northerner, save for four Democrats, supported it; every Southerner, regardless of party, opposed it. The next day, the congressional session's last, the Senate took no action on the amended bill. Thus Congress adjourned without passing the Wilmot Proviso.

Nor would Congress ever pass it. Nonetheless, for the next four years it repeatedly reemerged, and when it did a similar sectional voting pattern reappeared. It would pass the House, which Northerners dominated, only to die in the Senate, where free and slave states had equal representation and a few northern Democrats always voted with Southerners against it. By 1849 fourteen of fifteen northern state legislatures had passed resolutions instructing their state's U.S. senators (whom the legislatures rather than the public at large then elected) to impose the proviso on any territorial governments organized in lands taken from Mexico. By then, many Southerners had threatened to secede should the proviso ever be enacted. Clearly, the prospect of congressional prohibition of slavery from western territories split the nation's congressmen and large segments of public opinion along sectional lines; and the longer debate over it lasted, the more dangerous sectional animosity became. Wilmot, in sum, had completely opened Pandora's box. Within fifteen years the uncontainable evils unleashed would produce a terrible civil war.

That intensifying sectional animosity requires explanation. So does the fact that wrangling over slavery's possible extension into lands acquired from Mexico lasted until the Compromise of 1850 passed four full years after the proviso's introduction. Before undertaking such a discussion, however, we must examine the initial vote in 1846 and the reasons for it. That vote was extraordinary for two reasons. First, when Wilmot introduced his proviso, the war with Mexico was not yet three months old. Fighting would drag on until September 1847, when General Winfield Scott's American army captured Mexico City. And another six months would pass before the Senate ratified the Treaty of Guadalupe Hidalgo, which ended the war and actually ceded former Mexican soil to the United States. By then, many votes on the proviso had constantly provoked the same sectional pattern. Long before any territory was in fact acquired from Mexico, Northerners and Southerners had been polarized over the proviso. Why did the hypothetical prospect of future slavery extension or congressional prohibition of it ignite such sectional animosity when the war itself did not?

From May 1846 until the spring of 1848, in fact, debate on the war in party newspapers, in state and local party platforms, and on the floor of Congress was partisan, not sectional, just as arguments over Texas annexation had been. Democrats defended the war and Polk's project of taking territory from Mexico. By 1848, indeed, some southern Democrats had demanded the acquisition of the entire Republic of Mexico, a demand that clearly raised the stakes about the possible extension of slavery. In contrast, Whigs repeatedly denounced the war as an immoral act of aggression and an unconscionable landgrab, even as they praised Whig generals like Scott and Zachary Taylor for winning it.

The similar partisan alignments on the war and Texas annexation point to the second reason why the House vote on August 8, 1846, was so remarkable. In the final House vote on Texas annexation in late February 1845, every single Democrat had supported it and every Whig except one Southerner had opposed it, even though annexation clearly involved slavery extension. By the August 1846 vote on the Wilmot Proviso, which, again, applied to a wholly hypothetical acquisition of additional territory, northern Democrats and southern Whigs had dramatically shifted from their earlier stance. How can we explain those shifts, especially that of northern Democrats who were responsible for the proviso?

One must not discount the genuine personal antipathy of northern Democrats to slavery. Clearly, however, something had changed by the summer of 1846, for many of those same Democrats had unanimously supported the acquisition of Texas as a new slave state with the possibility that four additional slave states might be carved from it. One reason for the shift has already been alluded to—northern Democrats' fear of political disaster in the North should they appear to support a war waged to extend slavery still farther westward. Preston King, a Van Burenite Democrat from upstate New York, made this motivation crystal clear when he reintroduced the proviso into the House in January 1847. As soon as the war began, he explained, "the charge was iterated and reiterated that the war was undertaken on the part of the Administration, aided by the South, for the purpose of extending the area of slavery." To counter that charge, King wished to have some declaration that would "satisfy the northern people—satisfy the people whom we represent—that we are not to extend the institution of slavery as a result of this war."

Van Burenite northern Democrats like King, of course, had supported the final vote on Texas annexation only because they believed Polk had promised to renegotiate the terms to limit the size of the slaveholding area that was annexed. Their fury at Polk's betrayal, so succinctly captured in John Dix's reference to "the Texas fraud," by itself can explain their support for the proviso. The freshman Wilmot was himself a Van Buren man who, like Preston King, later accompanied Van Buren's defection to the Free-Soil Party.

Many other northern Democrats, however, were not Van Buren men. Most Pennsylvanians had never trusted him, and Midwesterners had enthusiastically embraced the expansionist planks of Democrats' 1844 national platform. Yet in the summer of 1846 those Democrats were also ready to revolt against the duplicitous Polk and the southern Democrats on whose behalf they believed he acted. They backed the proviso to demonstrate that northern Democrats must not be trifled with. Short-term political revenge, in short, helps explain northern Democrats' initial support for the proviso, although a healthy respect for northern public opinion clearly explains their continued support for the proviso when it came up again for congressional votes.

Polk had more than earned their rancor. During the 1844 presidential campaign, he had sent Philadelphia Democrats an ambiguously worded public pledge to retain the high protective tariff that Whigs, along with Pennsylvania Democrats, had passed in 1842. Armed with this ambiguous letter, Democrats in Pennsylvania and New Jersey campaigned in 1844 as that tariff's staunchest defenders and brazenly "dare[d] the Whigs to repeal it." Thus, when Congress met in December 1845 and the Polk administration moved immediately to lower the tariff, as Polk had privately assured Southerners he would during the 1844 campaign, Democrats from those two states felt egregiously betrayed by a slaveholding President intent on helping the South at their expense.

Midwestern Democrats were equally infuriated by Polk's apparent duplicity on the Oregon question. According to an 1818 Anglo-American treaty that was renewed in 1827, the so-called Oregon Country, which extended northward from the forty-second parallel to fifty-four degrees forty minutes, or the southern boundary of Alaska, was to be open in its entirety for joint settlement by British and American settlers. Americans had moved west over the Oregon Trail and settled almost entirely south of the Columbia River, the border between the modern states of Oregon and Washington. The Democratic platform of 1844 had called for the "reoccupation of Oregon . . . at the earliest practicable period," and midwestern Democrats enthusiastically embraced that call. Exactly what those words meant was another matter, but midwestern Democrats assumed they meant an end to joint occupation and American acquisition of the entire Oregon Country.

Polk himself had no such grandiose ambition. He mostly wanted American ports on the Pacific, to facilitate trade with Asia. Because sandbars in the Columbia River blocked the establishment of a deepwater port on it, Polk sought to extend the forty-ninth parallel, which divided Canada from the United States between the Great Lakes and the Rocky Mountains, to the Pacific Ocean. This extension would give the United States the modern state of Washington and with it a deepwater port on Puget Sound. For years, Polk's predecessors had pressed that settlement. For years, the English had rejected it on the perfectly accurate grounds that virtually all American settlers in the Oregon Country were south of the Columbia. If Oregon were to be divided between England and the United States, they maintained, the Columbia River should be the boundary.

To end this stalemate, Polk decided to bluff. He demanded American occupation of the entire Oregon Country, hoping that the British would then compromise on the forty-ninth parallel. He did so in his inaugural address and his first annual message to Congress in December 1845. In the latter document, he called on Congress to pass a resolution giving Great Britain the one-year notice for the end of joint occupation as stipulated in the Anglo-American Convention of 1818. He also asked Congress to build a series of forts along the Oregon Trail in case military action was necessary. Polk's bluff worked. In 1846 a treaty which ceded that part of the Oregon Country south of the forty-ninth parallel to the United States was signed and ratified.

The problem was that Polk never told congressional Democrats that he was bluffing. He wanted to use congressional cries to take all of Oregon as pressure to force the British to compromise. Several prominent midwestern Democratic senators, for the first time, raised the famous call "Fifty-four Forty or Fight" to demand the seizure of the entire Oregon Country from England. Whigs, who on principle opposed territorial expansion, especially as a result of war, denounced the calls. So, too, did southern Democrats. They could acquiesce in acquiring all of Oregon, but not if it required a war against England, southern cotton planters' biggest customer. John C. Calhoun, the proslavery exponent of Texas annexation and senator from South Carolina, led southern Democrats' antiwar forces. Hence, when Polk sent Congress the treaty with England dividing Oregon at the forty-ninth parallel, midwestern Democrats felt doubly betrayed. They were infuriated at Polk, who had misled them, and at southern Democrats, who refused to fight for all of Oregon after they had gone for all of Texas. That Polk sent his Oregon Treaty to the Senate on exactly the same day, August 8, 1846, that he asked for an appropriation to acquire still more south-western territory from Mexico, into which slavery might expand, and only three days after he had vetoed a rivers-and-harbors bill avidly sought by Midwesterners, only compounded their fury at Polk and what they called "the Slave Power." Their vote for Wilmot's proviso was, in part, the result.

Short-term anger at Polk and other southern Democrats in Congress helps explain northern Democrats' initial support for Wilmot's inflammatory proviso. But northern and southern public opinion best explains the continuing sectional polarization over it. Unlike members of Congress and delegates to the political parties' quadrennial national nominating conventions, the vast majority of Northerners and Southerners in the 1840s and 1850s never laid eyes on someone from the other section, let alone quarreled with him face-to-face. But newspapers and political speakers kept the citizenry abreast of partisan and sectional confrontations in Congress. The longer and more fractious congressional debate over the Wilmot Proviso became, the more intense sectional animosity in the population at large grew, which in turn unquestionably aggravated politicians' disagreement over that issue.

Northerners opposed slavery extension in the 1840s for a number of reasons. Condemning slaveholding as outrageously immoral, some hoped that blocking slavery's expansion would put it on the road to "ultimate extinction," as Abraham Lincoln later phrased it. The assumption here was that slavery was an economically inefficient institution and that plantation agriculture constantly needed fresh western land. Hence, the argument went, if slavery's expansion were prohibited, slavery in the exist-ing slave states would grow increasingly unprofitable, and slaveholders themselves would eventually emancipate their slaves to escape the economic burden of supporting them. Modern economic historians have demonstrated that this assumption was false, but as is so often the case in American history, perception mattered more than reality. And for those Northerners inspired by deep moral antipathy to slavery, its extension under any circumstances was unacceptable.

In this regard, a special feature of any possible acquisition of territory from Mexico was absolutely crucial to northern antislavery men. Unlike Texas, where slavery was already legal, Mexico had abolished slavery. To allow the reestablishment of slavery in an area previously emancipated struck many Northerners as an unconscionable and unforgivable sin. To make sure that horror never happened, they enthusiastically embraced Wilmot's proviso.

Far more Northerners opposed slavery's extension because they believed that their own social and economic system based on free labor required fresh western lands. Convinced that northern farmers, artisans, and wageworkers could not compete fairly with slaveholders whose workforce went unpaid, they argued that the two labor systems could not coexist in the same area. Thus they insisted on stopping slavery extension to preserve the West for the exclusive settlement of non-slaveholders like themselves.

Many northern whites also wanted to keep slaves out of the West in order to keep blacks out. The North was a pervasively racist society where free blacks suffered social, economic, and political discrimination; some midwestern states, indeed, legally banned the entry of blacks within their borders. Bigots, they sought to bar African-American slaves from the West. Wilmot himself proudly and repeatedly called his measure the "White Man's Proviso."

As had been the case during the fractious debates over Missouri's admission as a slave state and Texas's annexation, however, Northerners also wanted to stop slavery expansion in order to limit the growth of the South's power in national politics. Northerners increasingly condemned the so-called Slave Power as unceasingly aggressive, insatiably greedy for still more representatives and senators, and increasingly hostile to public policies that might benefit the North. Railing against the possible annexation of Texas in April 1844, Ohio Whig congressman Joshua R. Giddings, for example, complained: "To give the south the preponderance of political power would be itself a surrender of our Tariff, our internal improvements, our distribution of the proceeds of public lands. In short it would be the transfer of our political power to the slaveholders." Giddings was succinct: "It is the most abominable proposition with which a free people were ever insulted."

Texas annexation under the terms of the Brown amendment in 1845, in fact, proved the final straw for virtually all northern Whigs and many northern Democrats as well. Denouncing Texas annexation as "an act of National sin and dishonor," Michigan's Whigs in their state platform of September 1845 fulminated at "the political ascendancy and rule of the Slave Power" and "the arrogant demands of the Slave States . . . [whose] power is so often put forth in remorseless sectional hostility to our free institutions." Resentment of the Slave Power clearly helped motivate Wilmot himself. "I am jealous of the *power* of the South," he later wrote. "The South holds no prerogative under the Constitution, which entitles her forever to wield the Scepter of Power in this Republic, to fix by her own arbitrary edict, the principles & policy of this government, to build up and tear down at pleasure."

To some degree, Southerners' reasons for opposing the proviso mirrored Northerners' reasons for supporting it, although it is essential to distinguish between the motives of southern Democrats and those of southern Whigs. As southern Democrats saw it, the North already outnumbered the South in the House of Representatives because its population was growing at a much faster rate. If Northerners also gained a decisive majority in the Senate through the admission of additional free states, they might someday attempt to pass a constitutional amendment abolishing slavery. Southerners could accept the admission of Iowa as a free state in 1846 and Wisconsin two years later because they only balanced the admission of Texas and Florida as slave states in 1845. Additional free states, however, were another matter altogether, and hence Southerners resisted congressional prohibition of slavery from territories out of which new states might be formed. Put succinctly, establishing slavery in the territories where it did not yet exist served as a threshold political defense of slavery where it did.

As well, a few Southerners, again almost all of them Democrats, did believe that slaveholding planters required fresh western lands to remain prosperous. In essence, they found the northern case against slavery extension too credible to risk. A relatively small number of these southern Democrats, consequently, actually contemplated trying to carry slaves westward into any new lands acquired from Mexico.

In contrast, overwhelming evidence indicates that most southern Whigs, whether ordinary citizens or elected politicians, did not. Nor, at least in the 1840s, were they interested in gaining more slave states to increase southern political power in Washington. Otherwise, they would never have been so united in their opposition to Texas annexation in 1844–45. From the beginning of 1847 until March 1848, moreover, southern Whigs joined their northern colleagues in insisting that no additional territory be taken from Mexico as a result of the war, a stance utterly incompatible with a yen for further slavery extension.

Throughout the 1840s and 1850s, in fact, southern Whigs were far less aggressive in demanding pro-slavery concessions from the North on slavery extension and far readier to seek a mutually satisfactory sectional compromise on that issue than were southern Democrats. This pattern of behavior is especially perplexing because in most slave states Whigs dominated the black-belt plantation regions with the heaviest concentrations of slaves. In contrast, the backbone of Democratic voting strength came from non-slaveholders in regions outside the black belt where both slaves and slaveholders were rare. At first glance, the pattern of behavior should have been exactly the opposite of what it was.

Several factors help explain this seeming paradox. First and foremost, most southern Whig voters and especially slaveholding voters had no interest in moving west. They were too established and successful where they already lived. Moreover, they were firmly convinced that slavery could never be profitably established in any new lands from Mexico. In early 1850, after three years of increasingly rancorous sectional quarreling in Congress over slavery's extension into former Mexican lands, for example, one exasperated southern Whig complained that the endless dispute was about "moonshine," for "no matter what you may do or omit to do at Washington, there will never be slavery in any new territory." "The whole question is an abstract one without any practical bearing," echoed a Louisiana Whig newspaper editor that year, "as there is not nor ever was any prospect for slavery in those territories." A few southern Democrats admitted the same thing, yet they were far more concerned about ensuring the continued growth of southern political power than were Whigs.

Political considerations, indeed, also help explain the partisan differences. For one thing, southern Democrats were far more vulnerable to pressure from South Carolina's pro-slavery extremists, who almost always insisted on shoring up slavery on the South's periphery, than were southern Whigs. In part, this was because Calhoun, who flirted with both the Whig and the Democratic Party but never unalterably committed himself to either, had a hard core of Democratic allies in many southern states. Significantly, these allies often resided in the black-belt areas Whigs normally controlled. They sought to agitate the slavery extension issue both to cut into the Whig vote in slave-holding areas and to challenge Democratic dominance of non-slaveholders from elsewhere in their states.

Much more important, however, southern Whigs and Democrats reacted to federal economic policy in sharply contrasting ways. Whigs were strongest in, and most Whig representatives and senators hailed from, the most commercially developed areas of the South. They were determined to extend the market economy into underdeveloped regions of their states. To do this, they embraced the Whig program of federal help in the form of subsidies, a lenient banking and currency policy that ensured cheap and ample credit, and in some cases high protective tariffs. Democrats, North and South, regarded these developmental policies as anathema. Thus, to obtain them, southern Whigs had to cooperate with northern Whigs. Accordingly, they were far more reluctant than southern Democrats, who wanted nothing from the federal government other than territorial expansion and further concessions on slavery, to offend their northern congressional colleagues by pressing for slavery extension, especially when they regarded that prospect as mere "moonshine."

If these factors help explain the different behavior of southern Democrats and southern Whigs on most aspects of the slavery extension question, however, they make southern Whigs' fervent opposition to the Wilmot Proviso seemingly more inexplicable. There were sharp partisan differences in the South on slavery extension, but Southerners united across party lines in their hatred of the proviso and their determination that it must never be enacted. Why?

One answer is that even slaveholders who had no intention of moving west believed they had an economic stake in the slavery extension issue. Slaves were more than a coerced labor force. They also represented a substantial capital investment by their white owners. The price of slaves on slave markets determined the value of those assets, and demand set the price. Thus anything that threatened future demand, as exclusion of slaveholders from the West may have done, could reduce the value of slaveholders' investments. To protect that value, slaveholders resisted congressional prohibition of slavery extension.

Equally if not more important, almost all southern Whigs, and many southern Democrats as well, saw the issue primarily in symbolic rather than substantive terms. Allowing Northerners in Congress to bar slavery from new territories by congressional statute struck them as a violation of Southerners' equal rights in the nation. If Northerners could carry their property—their horses, cattle, furniture, and so on—into U.S. territories that were the common property of both sections, Southerner after Southerner protested for four years, it was insultingly unfair to bar Southerners from taking their chattel-slave property into those same areas on equal terms. By supporting Wilmot's hateful proviso, Southerners railed, Northerners were attempting to treat Southerners as inherently unequal to themselves. For any Southerner to acquiesce in such tyrannical treatment was to subordinate himself to northern dictation, effectively to become the willing "slave" of northern masters. This humiliation was something no self-respecting southern white man, Whig or Democrat, slaveholder or non-slaveholder, could ever tolerate.

Thus southern rhetorical denunciations of Wilmot's proviso rarely talked about actually extending slavery farther west. They rang, instead, with talk of impending degradation, inequality, and political enslavement to the northern majority. From Southerners' perspective, Wilmot's proviso did not primarily stymie slavery extension. It threatened their manhood, their rights, their equality, and their political liberty. Southern Whigs, no less than southern Democrats, utterly refused to submit to this abominable affront to personal and sectional honor.

Three examples of southern rhetoric suffice to illustrate Southerners' outrage. Peter V. Daniel, a Virginia Democrat and associate justice on the U.S. Supreme Court, complained that the proviso was based on a view that "pretends to an insulting exclusiveness or superiority on the one hand, and denounces a degrading inequality or inferiority on the other; which says in effect to the Southern man, Avaunt! You are not my equal, and hence are to be excluded as carrying a moral taint with you."

In support of resolutions he had introduced against the proviso, Calhoun thundered on the Senate floor in February 1847: "I say, for one, I would rather meet any extremity upon earth than surrender one inch of our equality . . . What! Acknowledge inferiority! The surrender of life is nothing to sinking down into acknowledged inferiority."

At the start of the portentous congressional session of 1850, Georgia Whig Senator John M. Berrien, who had voted against Texas annexation in 1844–45 every time he had the chance and stridently opposed taking any territory from Mexico, wrote to a Georgia kinsman about the continuing determination of northern Whigs to impose the proviso on the Mexican Cession: "I do not believe they would abolish slavery if they had the opportunity . . . but if they can confine it within its present limits, they will accomplish the double purpose of enjoying the benefit of the products of slave labor, and of obtaining such a preponderance in the councils of the nation, as will give the control of the Government entirely to them. Slavery will then exist in a double aspect. The African, and his owner, will both be slaves. The former, will as now, be the slave of his owner, but that owner, in all matters within the sphere of federal jurisdiction, will be the doomed thrall of those with whom he associated on the basis of equal rights."

The prospect of insulting inferiority to and political enslavement by the northern majority, along with the potential future danger to the security of slavery itself, made the proviso an explosive issue in the South. That is why Southerners increasingly threatened to secede from the Union should it ever be enacted. Many Southerners, certainly the vast majority of southern Whigs, cared far more about defending their section's equal rights on the territorial issue than about extending slavery into any new territories. Conversely, most Northerners cared far more about stopping slavery extension than about the precise method of doing so. Aware by early 1847 that the sectional polarization over the proviso threatened the national unity of their political parties necessary to enact legislation and conduct the impending presidential election of 1848, elected politicians saw room for maneuver. If they had escalated sectional tensions through their votes on the proviso, they might defuse that explosive animosity and end any danger to the Union by providing alternative methods to handle the slavery extension issue.

Calhoun offered one alternative to Wilmot's proviso that neither party seriously considered. A nominal Democrat at best during the 1840s, Calhoun had never trusted either major party as offering adequate protection to slavery or Southern Rights.

For years, in fact, his goal had been to eradicate party divisions in the South and combine all Southerners in a united sectional phalanx that could extort pro-slavery concessions from the North. Seizing on southern resentment about the proviso, he revived this project in 1847 by offering Senate resolutions that were the polar opposite of the proviso. Slavery followed the flag, insisted Calhoun. The Constitution itself legalized slavery in every square foot of territory possessed by the United States. No additional local or federal laws were necessary to establish it in those territories, but neither could Congress or the residents of those territories bar slavery from them. It was, according to Calhoun, flatly unconstitutional for them to do so. Calhoun's formula, in short, utterly flouted Northerners' hopes of blocking slavery extension. For politicians seeking to reunite their sectionally divided national parties, it was a nonstarter.

Democrats instead touted two possible solutions as fairer than either Wilmot's or Calhoun's. Some, including Polk's Secretary of State, James Buchanan, an aspirant for his party's 1848 presidential nomination, and eventually Polk himself, urged the extension of the Missouri Compromise line west of the Rocky Mountains all the way to the Pacific coast, where it would have ended near the modern town of Carmel, California. As in the Louisiana Territory, slavery would be prohibited north of that line. South of it slavery would be allowed but not explicitly established by congressional statute.

If only because it was unclear throughout 1847 and early 1848 how much, if any, territory would be taken from Mexico, most Democrats favored a different alternative. Known as popular sovereignty, this held that Congress should pass no law either prohibiting slavery from or establishing it in new western territories. Instead, the settlers in the territories should decide on slavery extension for themselves. Popular sovereignty, southern Democrats cheered, would spare Southerners from enactment of the hated proviso and initially allow slaveholders equal access with Northerners to common territories. It would protect, not deny, southern equality. At the same time, northern Democrats assured Northerners, popular sovereignty would stop slavery expansion just as surely as the proviso. That, Democrats cooed, was because non-slaveholders were certain to move more quickly and in greater numbers into the territories than were slaveholders. Those non-slaveholders would then bar slavery from them.

Democrats could make these contrasting promises about the benefits of popular sovereignty for the North and the South only because they were carefully ambiguous about precisely when, during the territorial stage, the decision about slavery would occur. Northern Democrats insisted it would be made by the territorial legislature, which could be elected as soon as the territory had five thousand residents. Southerners, in contrast, repeatedly declared that it would be made only after the territory had the sixty thousand residents necessary to write a constitution and apply for statehood. Until then, southern Democrats maintained, slaveholders would have every legal right to enter that territory. As past experience demonstrated, moreover, once slaveholders established a foothold in a territory, it always became a slave state when it entered the Union.

Democrats never rallied completely behind popular sovereignty as an alternative to the proviso. Calhoun's southern Democratic allies denounced it as unconstitutional because it might allow territorial residents to bar slavery and announced that they would never support a Democratic presidential candidate who embraced either the proviso or popular sovereignty. Increasingly, extremists like Alabama's William Lowndes Yancey called for Southerners to abandon both the Democratic and Whig parties for a new sectional alignment. In New York and other northern states, in contrast, Van Buren's most loyal Democratic supporters like Wilmot and Preston King clung to the proviso, dismissed popular sovereignty as a fraud that would allow slavery to enter lands that under Mexican law were free, and attacked any Northerners who embraced it as pro-southern doughfaces who would sell out northern interests and values.

Their contempt for popular sovereignty intensified after December 1847. That month Senator Lewis Cass of Michigan, whom Van Buren men detested as being primarily responsible for blocking Van Buren's nomination in 1844, issued a public letter endorsing popular sovereignty as the best solution for the slavery extension issue. A rival of Buchanan's for the Democrats' 1848 presidential nomination (Polk had promised shortly after his election in 1844 that he would not seek reelection), Cass went even further to woo southern support. He denounced the Wilmot Proviso as unconstitutional, and he pledged that if he was elected President, he would veto it should Congress ever pass it. From that point on northern Democrats split openly on votes over slavery extension in Congress and in northern state legislatures. Cass eventually won the Democratic nomination. Despite the utter silence of the Democratic national platform about slavery extension and despite the bolt of both New York's Van Burenite delegates and Alabama's Yancey from the convention in protest against Cass's success, the Democratic Party appeared committed to popular sovereignty as its solution to the territorial question going into the 1848 presidential campaign.

Whigs united much more easily than did Democrats on an alternative policy to the proviso, but their panacea proved much more short-lived. In early 1847 two Georgia Whigs, John Berrien in the Senate and Alexander H. Stephens in the House, simultaneously introduced resolutions stating that no territory whatsoever should be taken from Mexico as a result of the war.

With Democrats, who insisted on additional territorial acquisitions, still in control of both congressional chambers, Whigs had no prayer of ever adopting these resolutions. But the Georgians had hit upon a brilliant formula for reuniting their party and differentiating it from that of the Democrats. Thus Whig heavyweights in the Senate like Daniel Webster of Massachusetts and Ohio's Tom Corwin, whom northern antislavery Whigs were then booming for the party's 1848 presidential nomination because of his ferocious speeches against the Mexican War, quickly embraced it. The No Territory proposal had something for all Whigs. As a party, Whigs had traditionally opposed territorial expansion whether or not it involved slavery's extension. Better yet, No Territory rendered the Wilmot Proviso irrelevant, for if no Mexican territory was acquired, there was no need to adopt it. Thus the South would be spared an intolerable insult, and the North would block slavery's further extension. Throughout 1847, during most of which Congress was not in session, therefore, northern and southern Whigs rallied behind No Territory.

Convinced that slavery could not exist in any future acquisitions and that Northerners were determined to impose the proviso on them, southern Whigs outside Washington quickly saw the advantages of the new formula for their party, their section, and their nation. "Can a contest be imagined more frightful and furious than that which this very acquisition of Mexican Territory will excite between the North and South?" queried a Georgia Whig newspaper when endorsing No Territory in the spring of 1847. Tennessee's future Whig governor, William B. Campbell, concurred at the end of that year. "The North have the power in Congress," he wrote, "and if Mr. Polk gets territory by treaty, will it not be far worse for the South, and better that no territory had been acquired than that it should be admitted as free states."

Most northern Whigs continued to insist that the proviso be applied to any new territories, should they be acquired, but they, too, preferred to block territorial acquisition altogether. "We deprecate a war of conquest," declared the Ohio Whigs' January 1848 state platform, "and strenuously oppose the forcible acquisition of Mexican Territory; but, if additional territory be forced upon us, or acquired by the nation, we shall demand that there shall be neither slavery nor involuntary servitude therein." Many northern Whigs candidly endorsed this stance as necessary to reunite the party for the impending presidential election of 1848. Because southern Whigs would never support any candidate who was committed to the proviso and northern Whigs would never support a candidate who was not, Ohio's Corwin argued in late 1847, "hence arises the great *necessity* of taking early and strong ground against any further acquisition, settle on *that*, & the Wilmot Proviso dies."

Aside from holding northern and southern Whigs together, No Territory, along with denunciations of "Mr. Polk's War," gave the Whigs a viable campaign issue. They did less well in the congressional and state contests of 1847 than in those of 1846 (which focused on Democrats' economic legislation), but they still won often enough to convert the Democrats' 143-to-77 House majority in the Twenty-ninth Congress to a 115-to-108 Whig majority in the Thirtieth Congress. By the end of 1847, Whigs had become absolutely convinced that the war and territorial acquisition would be the central issues of the 1848 presidential campaign and that they needed a candidate staunchly opposed to both.

The best evidence of Whigs' belief in the power of the No Territory issue for the 1848 election came in Henry Clay's speech in his hometown of Lexington, Kentucky, on November 13, 1847. Stunned and embittered by his narrow and unexpected defeat in 1844, Clay had since then sulked in retirement on his Ashland estate. Now he flayed almost everything about his triumphant opponent's war. Had he been in Congress in 1846, he averred, he would never have voted for men and supplies, because of Polk's spurious claim that Mexicans had started the war. Whigs, he declared, "are utterly opposed to any purpose like the annexation of Mexico" and "have no desire for the dismemberment of the Republic of Mexico, but wish only a just and proper fixation of the limits of Texas." As a Southerner, Clay dared not embrace the Wilmot Proviso; still, he made his opposition to slavery and slavery extension crystal clear. Among the resolutions he asked his audience to affirm, the last declared: "That we do positively and emphatically disclaim and disavow any wish or desire on our part, to acquire any foreign territory whatever, for the purpose of propagating Slavery, or of introducing slaves from the United States into such foreign territory."

Clay's reentry onto the public stage and what he said there were hardly accidental. Clay unquestionably regarded No Territory as the best way to end sectional strife over slavery's extension. Nonetheless, his Lexington address also illustrates again how politicians repeatedly exploited the slavery extension issue for political advantage. Clay intended his speech to launch his campaign for the Whigs' 1848 presidential nomination. Northern Whigs, who sought to block the nomination of General Zachary Taylor, had desperately beseeched him to run. After Taylor's heavily outnumbered forces had won an astonishing victory over Mexicans at the battle of Buena Vista on February 23, 1847, a Taylor-for-President boom had swept across the country. But southern Whigs particularly favored Taylor because he owned plantations and over a hundred slaves in Louisiana and Mississippi. Many northern Whigs, in turn, deeply objected to Taylor, and not just because of his slaveholding. They blanched at supporting a professional soldier who helped fight a war they regarded as immoral and unjustifiable. More important, Taylor had never cast a vote, let alone aligned with any political party before 1848. He now refused to identify himself as a Whig or commit himself to Whig principles. No one knew where he stood on territorial acquisition or slavery expansion, let alone traditional Whig economic programs.

Clay, in contrast to Taylor, was widely regarded as the "embodiment of Whig principles," and he intended his Lexington address to reassure northern Whigs that he stood with them on the new issues that had emerged since 1844—the war, territorial acquisition, and slavery extension. The slavery extension issue unleashed by the war with Mexico, in sum, played just as important a role in the jockeying for the Whigs' 1848 presidential nomination as it did among Democrats. For the last month of 1847 and first ten weeks of 1848, moreover, Clay's bold stance at Lexington appeared to work wonders. While Taylor's southern Whig supporters called Clay's antislavery remarks outrageous, northern Whigs, who would have a majority of delegates at the party's national convention, increasingly turned against Taylor and gravitated toward Clay. By early March 1848 he had become the front-runner for the nomination.

The Senate's ratification of the Treaty of Guadalupe Hidalgo on March 10, 1848, shattered Clay's prospects and, apparently, those of the Whig Party as well. By that treaty America ended the war and acquired the huge Mexican Cession. Thus Whigs stood stripped of both the antiwar and No Territory issues they had expected to be the centerpiece of their campaign. Worse still from their perspective, Democrats could now run on a platform of peace, prosperity, and a successful war that along with Polk's Oregon Treaty of 1846 almost doubled the size of the United States. Simultaneously, Democrats could flay Whigs as unpatriotic naysayers who had opposed the war and territorial expansion. In response, some northern Whigs immediately abandoned Clay and instead boomed the war's other Whig military hero, Winfield Scott, for the Whig nomination in order to neutralize the war issue.

Whigs' real problem now that territory had been acquired, however, was the slavery extension issue. Throughout 1847, northern Whigs had committed themselves to imposing the proviso on any new acquisitions while pillorying Democratic proponents of popular sovereignty as pro-southern doughfaces. Yet as moderate northern Whigs had long been aware, southern Whigs could never accept a candidate openly committed to the hated proviso. The proviso still had the capacity to divide both parties along sectional lines. Witness the futile efforts of Congress to organize a formal territorial government for Oregon after its acquisition in August 1846. No one expected that slavery would enter Oregon. Yet Northerners in the House repeatedly insisted on attaching the proviso to any bill for Oregon. Southerners in the Senate repeatedly buried the tainted legislation. Thus bitter wrangling over imposing the proviso on the new Mexican Cession seemed assured.

Some Whig strategists saw a way out. As early as March 19, only nine days after the Senate ratified the treaty, a New York Whig congressman wrote his state party's leader that what the Whigs needed was a candidate who had not yet taken any public position on the proviso and could remain mum on it throughout the campaign. That way, he could be run one way in the North and a different way in the South. Because Taylor owned so many slaves, he advised, Taylor would have to endorse the proviso to carry the North and thus lose the South. The man for Whigs was Scott, who could remain absolutely mum because he owned no slaves.

At a bitterly divided national convention, where Northerners and Southerners almost came to blows, Taylor, rather than Scott, won the Whigs' nomination. He did so in part because prior to the convention he had released a public letter identifying himself as a Whig who was committed to at least one Whig principle, that presidents must not veto congressional legislation unless it was clearly unconstitutional. Eschewing any national platform, Whigs then launched the cynical two-faced campaign on the slavery extension issue. Southern Whigs argued that no large slaveholder like Taylor would ever betray the South by signing the hated Wilmot Proviso into law. As a national military hero, moreover, Taylor would restore harmony between the feuding sections and end northern assaults on southern rights and equality. In sum, southern Whigs stressed the defense of southern equality, not the physical extension of slavery into the Mexican Cession. In the North, Whigs stressed Taylor's apparent pledge not to veto congressional legislation. The best way to stop slavery expansion, they insisted, was to elect northern Whig congressmen who would enact the proviso, which Taylor would sign.

Democrats ran their own Janus-faced campaign. Southerners trumpeted Lewis Cass's pledge to veto the intolerable proviso, warned that Taylor might in fact sign it as northern Whigs promised, and lauded Democrats' achievement in gaining new territory into which slavery might expand. Northern Democrats iterated their argument that popular sovereignty could stop slavery extension just as effectively as the proviso without destroying the Union. They also stressed that their candidate was a Yankee while Whigs were running a slaveholder. In the South, in sum, both parties promised to deflect the insulting proviso. In the North, both promised to stop slavery's extension into the Mexican Cession.

Neither the major parties' nominees nor their campaigns

pleased adamant antislavery men in the North. Van Buren's devoted New York followers hated Cass. Upon his nomination
they bolted the Democratic national convention, returned angrily to New York, and nominated Van Buren as their own presidential candidate on a platform committed to barring slavery
from all territories by congressional statute. Ardent antislavery
Whigs, especially numerous in Ohio and Massachusetts, had
long threatened to leave the Whig Party if it nominated another
slaveholder. Meanwhile, supporters of the Liberty Party, which
had run an independent antislavery presidential candidate in
1840 and 1844, nominated their own candidate again in late
1847. But their most prominent leaders sought a broader
antislavery fusion with disaffected Democrats and Whigs.

In June 1848, after the Whig and the Democratic conventions,
Ohio's Liberty leaders called all Northerners committed to the
proviso and unhappy with Cass and Taylor to assemble in Buffalo
in August. Attended by over ten thousand men in an atmosphere
resembling an ecstatic religious revival, that gathering formed the
Free-Soil Party. Delegates nominated Van Buren for President and
Charles Francis Adams, leader of Massachusetts's most ardent
antislavery Whigs (or Conscience Whigs, as they were dubbed),
for Vice President. They also adopted a platform pledged to barring slavery from all territories by congressional law and preventing the admission of any more slave states into the Union. This
new party stood pledged to the principles of Wilmot's proviso
and to continued opposition to slavery expansion, no matter what
happened to the Mexican Cession. Free-Soilers' determination
to agitate against slavery extension, regardless of attempts to settle that issue, is one reason why that vexatious and increasingly
dangerous question defied permanent settlement. Just as clearly,
however, the undermining of Whigs' No Territory formula by
acquisition of the Mexican Cession is another.

Even before the Free-Soil convention met in August, northern Democrats and especially northern Whigs, who considered Taylor unlikely to carry the North, worried that the new party might attract their northern electorates. In desperation, Whigs, led by Senator John M. Clayton of Delaware, sought to resolve the entire territorial question so as to negate any rationale for a Free-Soil Party and still hold northern and southern Whigs together behind Taylor's candidacy. That effort failed. Its failure illustrates just how perplexingly difficult and divisive the slavery extension question had become by the summer of 1848.

At that time, Congress had still not organized a formal territorial government for Oregon, because of the sectional impasse over attaching the Wilmot Proviso to it. Instead, residents of Oregon, without congressional authorization, had formed a provisional government that banned slavery. Furious Southerners in Congress refused to recognize its legitimacy. Clayton offered a plan, immediately dubbed the Clayton Compromise, that used the stalemate over Oregon as the crowbar to break up the logjam over slavery extension in all of Polk's new territories. His bill would establish a territorial government for Oregon, specifically allowing the provisional government's antislavery ban to remain in force until the new territorial legislature ruled for or against slavery. With Oregon, Clayton dodged northern Whigs' demand for the proviso in favor of the Democrats' formula of popular sovereignty. Nonetheless, everyone knew the new territorial legislature would bar slavery. Southerners would save face, but Oregon would be free soil.

Clayton also called for congressional organization of territorial governments for California and New Mexico. But his bill explicitly barred those governments from either establishing or prohibiting slavery. Instead, federal judges must decide. Any slave brought into those territories, Clayton proposed, could sue in federal territorial courts to see if slavery was legal there. Any decision by those local, federally appointed judges could be appealed directly to the Supreme Court for a final decision. Like popular sovereignty, Clayton's formula for the Mexican Cession would eschew any congressional action like imposition of the proviso. The federal judiciary, not territorial settlers, must decide on slavery extension.

Clayton passionately defended his bill as eminently fair to both sections. Nonetheless, Northerners and Southerners from both parties immediately attacked it for giving the advantage to the other section. Northerners complained that Clayton's plan would allow slaveholders to enter lands that had been free from slavery under Mexican law, and that any judges appointed by the slaveholder Polk were bound to rule that slavery was legal. Citing the continuing legal force of Mexico's antislavery statutes in the Cession until they were explicitly replaced by new congressional legislation, Southerners in turn complained that judges would declare slavery illegal in the Cession. Despite this opposition, Clayton's bill passed the Senate, but it was quickly tabled without further action in the House. Congressmen from both sections were too uncertain about what might happen were they to accept Clayton's formula.

Before it adjourned in August, Congress finally managed to organize a territorial government for Oregon with slavery barred from it, as the House's northern majority insisted. After a prolonged sectional struggle, three Southerners, including Missouri's antislavery Benton, joined all Northerners in the Senate majority to pass the House bill. Rather than acknowledging the legitimacy of imposing the proviso on Oregon, however, Polk stipulated that he signed the bill only because Oregon was north of the Missouri Compromise line. Nonetheless, while finally settling disputes over Oregon, Congress had failed to organize any civil governments in the vast Mexican Cession by the time it adjourned in the summer of 1848. Politicians' attention now turned exclusively to the fall elections.

Whig and Democratic maneuvers in Washington during July did nothing to deter the formation of the Free-Soil Party in August. Contrary to Whigs' fears, however, Van Buren's candidacy hurt Cass far more than it did the slaveholder Taylor. For one thing, many deeply antislavery Whigs in the North utterly refused to support Van Buren. To them, he epitomized everything they had hated about the Democratic Party since their own party's formation in 1834, especially his earlier pro-slavery concessions. For another, Van Buren's Free-Soil candidacy undercut southern Democrats' claims that Cass was safer for the South on the proviso issue than Taylor because Cass was overtly pledged to veto it. How, southern Whigs tellingly asked, could southern voters possibly trust Cass when Van Buren, a northern Democrat who had previously pledged to defend slaveholders' rights, was now leading an overtly anti-southern, antislavery party?

Some southern Democrats defected to the slaveholder Taylor's column in November, but far more simply abstained rather than vote for someone they could not trust on the slavery extension issue. As a result of the drop in Democratic turnout, Taylor carried eight slave states in 1848, compared with Clay's five in 1844. He also came startlingly close to winning traditional Democratic strongholds like Virginia, Alabama, and Mississippi.

Van Buren failed to carry a single northern state, but he amassed 291,000 northern votes (14 percent of the total), compared with the Liberty candidate's 63,000 (3 percent of the total) in 1844. Van Buren's vote varied widely from state to state in the North—it was minuscule in Pennsylvania and New Jersey, for example. He drew votes from both Democrats and Whigs, but ultimately his candidacy damaged Cass far more than Taylor. Defections by antislavery Whigs infuriated by Taylor's nomination handed Ohio to Cass. More often, Whig defections were proportionally greatest in states like Vermont and Massachusetts, where Whigs' traditional margin over Democrats was so large they still won, or in heavily Democratic states like Maine and New Hampshire that Whigs stood no chance of carrying. But Democratic defections to Van Buren in New York, where he garnered 120,000 of his total votes, gave the state's huge electoral vote, along with thirty-two of its thirty-four congressional seats, to the Whigs. Together with a renewed salience of economic issues by the fall of 1848 that swung Connecticut, Pennsylvania, and New Jersey into the Whig column, Democratic defections were enough to give seven free states and victory in the electoral college to Taylor.

Whigs won the presidency, a substantial majority of congressional elections, and three-fourths of the gubernatorial elections held in 1848. They did so in large part because of their deft two-faced stance on slavery extension. By promising in the North that Taylor would sign the proviso and pointing to Van Buren's hated pedigree as a Jacksonian Democrat, they had blunted the Free-Soil challenge and won a majority of the northern electoral vote. By raising doubts about Cass's purported fairness to the South and praising the slaveholder Taylor as the South's best defender, they had won a majority of the South's electoral and popular vote. But Whigs had elected a man who for most of 1847 and 1848 had presented himself as a "No Party" candidate who would not run a partisan administration and whose private ideas about how to deal with the vexatious slavery extension issue remained utterly unknown.

Equally important, the election had done nothing to resolve the sectional conflict over slavery's possible extension into the

Mexican Cession. Not only did the northern and southern wings of both major parties promise different outcomes to their respective electorates, but Congress had organized a territorial government for Oregon only after a titanic two-year struggle, and nothing whatsoever had been done by Washington authorities for the huge Mexican Cession.

3

THE COMPROMISE OF 1850

However successfully the Whig and Democratic parties had papered over their sectional divisions on slavery extension in 1847 and 1848, during the year following Taylor's election those divisions widened markedly and increasingly threatened the Union. Political decisions both inside and outside Washington measurably intensified animosity. At the same time, however, politicians' very attempt to exploit sectional antagonism for partisan gain reflected their constituents' deepening distrust and anger. By the end of 1849, sectional conflict over the fate of slavery in the Mexican Cession had come to seem more irresolvable and dangerous than ever.

In December 1848 lame-duck President James Polk sent his final annual message to Congress. It influenced debates over the Mexican Cession in three ways. First, Polk publicly recommended extension of the Missouri Compromise line, with slavery allowed south of it, to the Pacific coast. During 1849 and 1850 increasing numbers of southern Democrats would make that extension nonnegotiable. Second, Polk officially acknowledged that earlier in 1848 gold had been discovered in the hills of California northeast of San Francisco Bay. Rumors of the strikes had already filtered back east, but Polk's announcement helped trigger the legendary gold rush of 1849, when almost 100,000 fortune seekers flooded into the new American possession. This deluge was all-important. No federally recognized civil governments yet existed anywhere in the Mexican Cession. Military commanders exercised federal authority in California and New Mexico, while the Mormons who had moved to the area around the Great Salt Lake earlier in the decade governed themselves in splendid isolation. Military government was now woefully inadequate for California because there were insufficient troops to control its exploding civilian population. Civil government had to be established, and thus the sectional stalemate over Wilmot's proviso had to be confronted once again.

Third, Polk accompanied his message with a remarkable map purporting to show what the United States had acquired from Mexico. Because lawmakers had only the vaguest idea of southwestern geography, this map profoundly shaped subsequent proposals. Polk's mapmaker consigned everything east of the Rio Grande, including the New Mexican trading center of Santa Fe, to the slave state Texas—that is, not as part of the lands the federal government had acquired. Whigs had never recognized the Rio Grande as Texas's southwestern boundary. Several Whig-controlled northern state legislatures immediately responded to Polk's map by instructing their U.S. senators to fix Texas's western boundary at the Nueces River, hundreds of miles east of the Rio Grande. Polk's map depicted New Mexico as a narrow, cigar-shaped vertical strip on the west bank of the Rio Grande, running northward from El Paso on the south to the northern boundary of modern Colorado.

Everything else in the vast Cession, from the Pacific Ocean to the Rocky Mountains, was identified as California, Polk's great trophy from the war. On paper, the Mexican province of California had always encompassed more than what is now the state of California, but Mexican settlers along the West Coast, or Californios, as they were known, had never considered the largely unpopulated expanse east of the Sierra Nevada part of their domain. Nonetheless, when Washington policy makers confronted what to do with the Mexican Cession, they thought of California as this enormous region.

In response to Polk's map, Democratic Senator Stephen A. Douglas of Illinois, known as the "Little Giant" because of his short, muscular physique and powerful debating style, introduced a resolution calling for the immediate admission of the entire Mexican Cession, including the sliver Polk's mapmaker allotted to New Mexico, as the new state of California. Douglas favored organizing territories on a popular sovereignty basis, but his motive for having California skip the territorial stage is easily inferred. In 1848 the Free-Soil Party had made especially deep incursions into the Democratic vote in several midwestern states, most notably Wisconsin and Douglas's own Illinois. It seemed likely to attract even more converts the longer the debate over slavery in the territories lasted.

After Cass's defeat in 1848, moreover, Democrats in several northern states eagerly sought to woo back defectors to the Free-Soilers or even form coalitions with them against the victorious Whigs. Thus they disavowed popular sovereignty and reembraced congressional prohibition of slavery from all federal territories. In addition, in several northern states, including Illinois, Democratic state legislators joined with Free-Soilers and Whigs to instruct their states' senators to impose the proviso on the Cession. Douglas meant to destroy this Free-Soil leverage over northern politics with his California statehood bill.

Slavery was already barred from the remainder of the Louisiana

Territory not yet admitted to statehood. The huge Oregon Territory had been organized on a free-soil basis during the previous summer. Only in the Mexican Cession was the slavery question unresolved. Admitting it immediately as a single state would eliminate the territorial question entirely and eradicate any rationale for the continuation of the Free-Soil Party. As everyone in Washington that winter knew, California was certain to be a free state because Mexico's antislavery statutes still barred slaveholders from it. Precisely because southern senators recognized this fact, however, they buried Douglas's proposal in a hostile committee that refused to report it out for Senate action.

Shortly thereafter, Calhoun seized on Southerners' furious reaction to Northerners' attempt in the House to abolish the slave trade in the District of Columbia, an effort that eventually failed, to aggravate sectional tension. Calhoun summoned all Southerners in Congress to a caucus in early January to devise a united response to northern insults and aggression. Southern Whigs recognized Calhoun's call for precisely what it was: an attempt to disband political parties in the South and thus destroy the national Whig Party before Taylor's inauguration. Most Whigs, therefore, boycotted the caucus. When Calhoun, as its spokesman, issued an address to Southerners' constituents on February 4, most southern Democrats as well as southern Whigs considered it far too inflammatory. Only 48 of 124 Southerners in Congress signed it, and that minority included only two of forty-eight southern Whigs in the House and Senate.

Calhoun's Southern Address rehearsed a long litany of supposed northern aggressions against slaveholders' rights, starting with the adoption of the Missouri Compromise line in 1820. To right these wrongs, he demanded that slaveholders be given equal access with Northerners to the Mexican Cession. Far more ominously, he warned that northern aggressions were leading inevitably to the social cataclysm of abolition and that Southerners would be justified in using any method of resistance to avoid that horror. In short, he hinted that Southerners might secede unless the North retreated.

Calhoun's Southern Address had two crucial political consequences. Although only a minority of southern Democratic congressmen had signed it, it was clearly a Democratic document. Thus it reinforced southern political developments already in motion. Disgusted at their failure to carry slave states behind Cass's popular sovereignty doctrine, southern Democrats immediately abandoned it after November 1848 and instead began to demand equal access for slaveholders to all the Mexican Cession. They also ratcheted up their warnings that Taylor and other southern Whigs would betray the South by abetting enactment of the proviso. Southern Whig congressmen's refusal to sign the Southern Address, Democrats shouted, provided added evidence of impending Whig treachery. In the 1849 elections the charge proved lethal. Of the sixty congressional seats at stake in the South that year, Democrats won forty-one and Whigs only nineteen; in 1847, by contrast, the two parties had split them evenly, thirty-thirty. Seven slave states, four of which had been carried by Taylor in 1848, also held gubernatorial elections that year. Democrats won them all. By the end of 1849, southern Whigs had clearly been put on the defensive regarding slavery extension. That fact proved exceptionally important in the Thirty-first Congress, where Democrats would control the House as well as the Senate because of Whig defeats in 1849.

When Calhoun published his Southern Address in early February 1849, southern Whig congressmen already knew that southern Democrats planned to hammer them as untrustworthy on slavery extension during the impending elections. By then, moreover, they had also come to fear that the national Whig

Party, which they dearly hoped to preserve, stood in grave jeopardy. Both northern Whigs and Democrats seemed determined to impose the proviso on the Mexican Cession in order to deflect the Free-Soil political threat at home. If a few southern senators joined them, as they had the previous summer when establishing an antislavery government for the Oregon Territory, the proviso might actually pass the next Congress. If that happened on Taylor's watch, the Whig Party was doomed. If Taylor signed the proviso, southern Whigs would be routed. If, instead, he vetoed it, northern Whigs would be crushed at the polls. By February southern Whigs had become convinced that the salvation of the Whig Party required a settlement for the Mexican Cession before Taylor's inauguration.

Democrats controlled the Senate, so Whigs looked to the House, where they held the majority of seats. Virginia Whig William Ballard Preston, whom Taylor would shortly appoint as his Secretary of the Navy, introduced a modified version of Douglas's California statehood bill. The Preston bill, like Douglas's plan, would have vaporized the former Mexican province of New Mexico. It would extend the boundary of Texas some thirty miles west of the Rio Grande, thus pushing the area where slavery was legal slightly farther westward. The entire remainder of the Mexican Cession would then be immediately admitted as the state of California without any formal territorial stage to which the explosive Wilmot Proviso might be attached. Southern Whigs knew that Californians would prohibit slavery in any new state constitution, but that outcome seemed far more palatable than imposition of congressional prohibition by a dictatorial northern majority. Thus Georgia Whig Congressman Robert Toombs, who had worked assiduously to secure Taylor's nomination in 1848 and who within a year would vow to lead a secession movement in the South should Congress itself try to bar slavery from California, hymned praises to Preston's plan. Like many other southern Whigs, he believed that "it cannot be slave country." Therefore, "we have only the point of honor to save; and this will save it, and rescue the country from all danger of agitation."

Southern Whigs fully expected that the admission of a huge new free state would give their northern Whig colleagues sufficient political cover to blunt Free-Soil charges about Whigs' failure to organize territorial governments with slavery explicitly prohibited. Northern Whigs disagreed. When Preston's bill finally came up for a vote in late February, northern Whigs moved, and northern Democrats helped them adopt, an amendment barring slavery from the area before any state constitutional convention could be held. In this amended form, Preston's bill failed to receive a single favorable vote. Once again Congress adjourned without providing any civil governments for the Mexican Cession. Now Taylor and the new, Democratic-controlled Congress that would not meet until December 1849 had to devise an acceptable solution to the seemingly interminable quarrel over slavery's possible extension into the Mexican Cession.

When Zachary Taylor was inaugurated as President on March 5, 1849, no one knew his position on slavery extension, the Mexican Cession, or, indeed, any other concrete public policy. Nor did Taylor's unusually brief and barely audible inaugural address give a clue to his intentions. The doughty old soldier—and Taylor, it must be stressed, had been a professional soldier sworn by oath to uphold the Constitution and defend the nation throughout his entire adult life—had, in fact, provided hints as to what he might do in private letters to close friends and relatives during 1847 and 1848.

An avid nationalist, Taylor considered the explosive sectional conflict over the Wilmot Proviso the gravest threat to the United States since the American Revolution. An experienced, if usually absentee, slaveholding cotton planter who had traversed a swath of northern Mexico during his successful military campaigns of 1846 and 1847, he was also utterly convinced that no slaveholder in his right mind would attempt to carry slaves into that arid desert. Thus Taylor, like Toombs, believed that only honor was at stake for the South in the quarrel over slavery extension. Within weeks of his inauguration, Taylor, aided by his Secretary of State, Delaware's Clayton, set out to find a solution for the Mexican Cession that might satisfy both Northerners and Southerners.

Taylor astutely recognized that the Wilmot Proviso was the crux of the problem. Northern politicians now demanded it, if only to negate the Free-Soil Party's threat. Whatever Southerners thought about the prospect of actually carrying slaves into the Mexican Cession (and no one then had any idea that California would eventually become the leading producer of cotton and rice in the United States), they unalterably opposed congressional prohibition. Thus Taylor and Clayton quickly decided to skip a formal territorial stage entirely and create new state governments in the Cession. To avoid antislavery amendments like the one that killed Preston's bill, they would not ask Congress to give prior authorization for statehood movements. Instead, they would urge residents in the Mexican Cession to draw up state constitutions and apply for statehood while Congress was out of session between March and December 1849. That way, the new Congress in December would be presented with a fait accompli that bypassed a formal territorial stage.

Unlike Douglas and Preston, Taylor sought two new states, California and New Mexico. He dispatched an emissary to the American military commander in Santa Fe, ordering him to urge New Mexico's residents to write a constitution and apply for statehood. By itself, this action signaled that Taylor held no brief for Texas's claim to all the land east of the Rio Grande, and subsequently he rejected this claim more emphatically. Simultaneously, Taylor sent Thomas Butler King, a Georgia Whig congressman, to California by sea to urge its residents to write a new state constitution as well.

Nor did Taylor ignore the Mormon settlement around the Great Salt Lake that was within the borders of California according to Polk's map. He sent a third emissary there to urge the Mormons to send delegates to the California constitutional convention and become part of that new state. Every square inch of the Mexican Cession, if Taylor had his way, would elude formal territorial status and congressional wrangling over the proviso. Taylor and Clayton explicitly instructed their agents to say nothing about whether the new state constitutions should allow or prohibit slavery. Still, they fully expected that both documents would bar it. They also fully expected that both new states would send Whigs to the Senate, in gratitude for Whigs' facilitating their admission as states. By late April 1849 Clayton exulted to an ally, "As to California and New Mexico, I have been *wide awake* . . . The plan I proposed to you last winter will be carried out fully. The States will be admitted—free and Whig!"

In hindsight, Taylor's plan had much to recommend it. Since southern Whigs had rallied unanimously around the California statehood bill proposed by the Virginian Preston, they might support it. So, too, might some southern Democrats, especially those who had refused to sign Calhoun's belligerent Southern Address. To be sure, Taylor was proposing the admission of two new free states, but he was averting the imposition of the hated proviso. No northern Democrat dared vote against the admis-

sion of free states, once their constitutions reached Congress, and Taylor could offer northern Whigs a plan that blocked slavery from the entire Mexican Cession and thereby undercut the rationale for the vexatious Free-Soil Party. During a speech in northwestern Pennsylvania in late August, indeed, Taylor, without giving specific details of what he was up to, announced that "the people of the north need have no apprehension of the further extension of slavery . . . The necessity of a third party [that is, the Free-Soil Party] would soon be obviated."

During 1849, however, developments in the West did not go according to plan. Contrary to Taylor's wishes, residents of New Mexico did not immediately write a constitution to apply for statehood. Instead, they petitioned Congress to create a *territorial* government for them, with slavery explicitly barred and the former eastern boundary of the Mexican province on the Nueces River restored. This petition ensured precisely the congressional donnybrook over the proviso Taylor sought to avoid. Upon further prodding by Taylor in early 1850, New Mexicans did draft a new state constitution. By the time it was officially received in Washington, however, both Taylor and prospects of Congress's ever passing his plan were dead.

Astonishingly, given their deep suspicion of other Americans, Mormons agreed to Taylor's proposal to join the new state of California. They appointed some twenty men to accompany Taylor's agent John Wilson on the long and arduous overland trek to California to serve as delegates in its constitutional convention. By the time they reached the West Coast, however, that convention had long since completed its work and adjourned. The constitution it wrote claimed only the area west of the Sierra Nevada for California, leaving the Mormons and vast parts of the Mexican Cession in limbo and still subjects for vituperative sectional dispute.

On the day before Thomas Butler King landed in San Francisco, the military governor of California, on his own initiative, had called for a state constitutional convention to meet in September at Monterey. The constitution adopted there barred slavery and defined California's modern boundaries. After it was ratified in a popular referendum, the Californians sent it, along with the two Democratic senators they had elected, contrary to the hopes of Clayton and Taylor, to Washington for Congress's approval.

Taylor publicly revealed his plans for the first time in his December annual message and a more detailed special message to Congress on January 21, 1850. Once California's officially ratified constitution arrived, he urged, Congress should immediately admit it without any further conditions regarding slavery. New Mexico, he promised, would also soon send a constitution, and Congress should admit it too as a state when that document arrived. Making New Mexico a state, he argued in his latter message, would allow the Supreme Court to settle the boundary dispute with Texas. Aside from admitting these two states, Congress should do nothing else about the Mexican Cession. "By awaiting their action all causes of uneasiness may be avoided and confidence and kind feeling preserved," he insisted in December.

In January he was more explicit. His call for admitting California and New Mexico as states, without any other congressional action for the Cession, was meant "to remove all occasion for the unnecessary agitation of the public mind." Until the residents of New Mexico applied for statehood, they would continue to "enjoy the benefit and protection of their municipal laws originally derived from Mexico [that is, Mexico's antislavery statutes]," while residents in "the residue" of the Cession would also undoubtedly "settle all questions of domestic policy for themselves" when they applied for statehood. "Seeing, then, that the question which now excites such painful sensations in

the country will in the end certainly be settled by the silent effect of causes independent of the action of Congress," he hymned in conclusion, "I again submit to your wisdom the policy recommended in my annual message of awaiting the salutary operation of those causes, believing that we shall thus avoid the creation of geographical parties and secure the harmony of feeling so necessary to the beneficial action of our political system."

Congressmen reacted to Taylor's proposals in divergent ways that were shaped largely by eastern political developments since his inauguration. The few Free-Soilers in Congress (two in the Senate and some eight or nine in the House) raged at Taylor's thinly concealed attack on their party and its central doctrine. They would admit California as a free state, but they insisted on organizing territorial governments in the remainder of the Cession with slavery explicitly prohibited, on reducing the size of Texas, and on abolishing slavery itself, not just the public slave trade, in the District of Columbia.

Northern Whig congressmen, most of whom had been elected in 1848, were badly shaken by the results of the North's 1849 elections. Whigs had suffered outright losses or seen their popular and state legislative majorities sharply reduced at the hands of Democrats or coalitions of Democrats and Free-Soilers in virtually every northern state. Northern Whigs thus arrived in Washington in December 1849 determined to impose the proviso on any territorial governments Congress organized, lest Free-Soilers make further gains in 1850 at their expense. Many also demanded that Texas's western border be brought back to the Nueces River, thus reducing that part of the West in which slavery was legal. Equally important, they saw the speedy admission of New Mexico and California, so long as Mexican law barred slavery until they were admitted, as a way to trump Free-Soilers' insistence on organizing territorial governments with the proviso.

Thus northern Whigs became Taylor's biggest backers in the Thirty-first Congress. Their support was important. Democrats outnumbered Whigs in both chambers of Congress, but in the House that margin was fewer than ten votes, with Free-Soilers holding the balance of power. More important, in the House northern Whigs outnumbered their southern colleagues seventy-six to thirty, a fact that clearly shaped the content of Taylor's messages. By themselves or even in combination with Free-Soilers, northern Whigs could not pass legislation. But if they held together and were aided by northern Democrats, whose state parties had now recommitted themselves to the proviso, they could block any alternative to Taylor's plan that might allow slavery extension into the Mexican Cession.

Northern Democratic congressmen from districts with significant Free-Soil constituencies adopted the same stance as northern Whigs. Far more important, however, was a group of incumbent northern Democratic senators who had been sent to the Senate prior to the emergence of the Free-Soil Party in the summer of 1848 and who were ideologically committed to popular sovereignty. Of these, the most significant were Michigan's Lewis Cass, the party's 1848 standard-bearer; Illinois's Douglas; Indiana's Jesse D. Bright; Pennsylvania's Daniel Sturgeon; and especially New York's Daniel S. Dickinson, perhaps the single most influential individual in the entire Senate. Dickinson led New York's conservative Hunker Democrats, who had feuded for years over sundry policies and control of the state Democratic organization with Van Buren's allies (or Barnburners, as they were known in New York). In 1848 they stood steadfastly behind Cass and popular sovereignty when the Barnburners bolted to the Free-Soil Party.

These Democrats were appalled that local Democratic leaders in their home states had repudiated popular sovereignty, bargained with Free-Soilers, whom they despised as dangerous fanatics, and joined with other antislavery men in northern legislatures to instruct them to impose the proviso on the Mexican Cession. Events in Ohio the preceding winter especially worried them. Then Democrats in the Ohio state legislature had willingly dumped their former Democratic colleague William Allen from his Senate seat and elected the Free-Soiler Salmon P. Chase in return for Free-Soilers' help in securing Democratic control of the state legislature. Conservative Democratic senators such as Douglas, Dickinson, and Cass could too easily envision suffering a similar fate.

As these conservative Democrats reconvened in Washington during the winter of 1849–50, they agreed to exert their influence as party leaders to force Democratic state parties in New York, Pennsylvania, Ohio, Indiana, Michigan, Illinois, and other northern states to recant their recent re-embrace of Wilmot's proviso, repudiate cooperation with Free-Soilers, and rally again behind the Democrats' demand that territories be organized in the Cession on a popular sovereignty basis. All northern Democrats accepted Taylor's proposal to admit California as a free state, but the conservatives contemptuously rejected his plea for Congress to shun the creation of formal territorial governments in the remainder of the Mexican Cession. Instead, they insisted on organizing such territories on a popular sovereignty basis, both to reassert their own personal command over the Democratic Party's northern wing and to defy the Free-Soilers.

This bloc of northern Democratic senators had leverage over what Congress did with Taylor's proposal for yet another reason that, ostensibly, had nothing to do with slavery extension. Between March and December 1849, Taylor and his cabinet managed to infuriate virtually the entire congressional wing of the Whig Party by their unfathomably maladroit dispensation of

federal patronage appointments of postmasters, customs collec-
tors, U.S. marshals, and other positions. By the fall of 1849 many
Whigs had begun to clamor for Taylor to replace his entire cabinet, while Whig representatives and senators had publicly
vowed to secure Senate rejection of Taylor's nominees when
they came up for confirmation in 1850. To do so, however, they
had to work with Democrats, who controlled the Senate. And
the Democratic senators with the most say on confirmations
were precisely the Northerners who wanted to organize territorial governments in the remainder of the Mexican Cession outside California on a popular sovereignty basis.

During the unprecedentedly long first session of the Thirty-
first Congress, the Senate's Democratic majority deliberately
delayed any action on Taylor's nominees for federal jobs until
August and September, when the Senate and House finally
voted on proposals for the Mexican Cession. They sought to
maximize pressure on northern Whigs, who cared deeply about
who received the patronage plums in their home states. The
price for help on patronage decisions, Democrats bluntly told
northern Whigs in Congress, was the organization of territorial
governments without the proviso, precisely what northern
Whigs had promised their voters since 1846 that they would
never allow.

Ultimately, however, what gave northern Democratic senators committed to popular sovereignty so much leverage on
what the Senate and therefore Congress did with Taylor's plan in
1850 was the need they and southern Whigs perceived to con-
ciliate the South on the slavery extension issue. In February
1849, Georgia's Robert Toombs had defended Preston's California statehood bill as perfectly fair to the South since it pro-
tected southern honor and slavery could not exist in California.
Within two months of his return to Georgia after Congress ad-

journed, however, he wrote to Preston that "public feeling in
the South is much stronger than many of us supposed." He was
now convinced not only that "passage of the Wilmot Proviso
would lead to civil war" but also that Southerners would react
to California statehood "with bitterness of feeling & without
cordiality" if slavery was excluded from it. Democrats' charges
that Whigs would betray the South on the slavery extension issue helped create this angry mood. When word reached the
South about Taylor's August speech in Pennsylvania, Southerners inferred that Taylor now intended to sign the proviso should
Congress pass it. Taylor's speech, consequently, worsened the
Whigs' debacle in the remaining southern elections of 1849. After trouncing the Whigs in November, Mississippi's Democrats
issued a call for a region-wide southern convention to meet in
Nashville, Tennessee, in June 1850. The purpose would be to
devise a common response if Congress had passed the proviso
by then. Many suspected that that response would be secession.
Meanwhile, in Georgia, where Democrats had routed Whigs in
the October elections, Democratic legislators in December
pushed through resolutions instructing Democratic Governor
George Towns to call a secession convention immediately if the
new Congress enacted the proviso, admitted California as a free
state, or failed to pass a new, more rigorous fugitive-slave act.

Like Northerners' increasing demand for abolishing the District of Columbia's slave trade, the call for a new fugitive-slave
law was not directly related to the struggle over slavery extension. Taylor, indeed, had omitted any reference to either demand in his messages to Congress. Nonetheless, slaveholders,
who faced increasing difficulty in recapturing runaways in the
North because northern public authorities refused to assist
them, had been pressing for a new law for years. What was un-
usual about Georgia's resolution was that it called the failure to

pass such a law grounds for secession. Given that the vast majority of escaped slaves who made it into the North came from the upper South, not the lower South, Georgia's ultimatum suggests a stacking of the deck to justify secession.

Without question, the actions by Mississippi and Georgia in late 1849 reflected a more defiant and dangerous temper in the lower South. When Georgia Whig Alexander Stephens reached Washington in December 1849, he complained that neither northern Whigs nor Taylor's administration had any idea how explosive "the excitement in the South on the Slavery question" had become over the preceding year. Furious that "insolent and unyielding" northern Whigs refused "to calm and quiet" the South's "feelings," Stephens, Toombs, and four other southern Whigs bolted the party's initial organizational caucus when it refused to disavow the proviso. They also refused to support the Whigs' candidate for House Speaker since he was a Northerner. To justify that stand, Toombs angrily warned northern Whigs on the House floor, "If by your legislation you seek to drive us from the territories of California and New Mexico" or "to abolish slavery in this District . . . *I am for disunion* and . . . I will devote all I am and all I have on earth to its consummation."

The intensification of southern resentment meant that few southern congressmen could or would support Taylor's plan. By itself, California's admission would upset the precious sectional balance of power in the Senate and was thus intolerable to Democrats. Most southern Democrats, indeed, considered Mexico's antislavery statutes, if allowed to remain in place as Taylor urged, as pernicious as the proviso. The only acceptable solution for the Mexican Cession, most southern Democrats insisted, was to prevent California statehood and extend the Missouri Compromise line to the Pacific coast, with slavery explicitly legalized by congressional law in the area south of it, from Texas to the Pacific.

This Democratic assault meant that the few southern Whigs left in Congress risked political annihilation at home if they supported Taylor's plan. At the same time, however, almost all southern Whigs deplored Democratic threats of secession. They yearned for a compromise solution. Still convinced that slavery would never be established in any part of the Cession, they could accept statehood for California if Southerners won more concessions in the remainder of the Cession than Taylor's plan offered.

Simultaneously, Southerners' threats of secession allowed northern Democrats, who also accepted statehood for California, to justify their insistence on organizing territorial governments with popular sovereignty as absolutely necessary for *"the preservation & perpetuity of the Union."* Here were the seeds of the pro-compromise coalition of northern Democrats and southern Whigs that emerged in 1850. They would wage legislative combat against northern Whigs and Free-Soilers, who opposed any pro-southern concessions, and against southern Democrats, who denounced any proposal that admitted California. The alignments in 1850, in fact, differed from any previous congressional divisions over slavery extension. Both major parties split along sectional lines. Yet within each section's delegation, distinct partisan differences remained. Rival parties in each section still reflexively opposed each other in order to establish distinctive platforms on which to campaign.

Because only northern Whigs fully supported Taylor's plan but lacked the votes to pass it, Taylor's messages ignited a search by Congress to develop its own policy. The first person to offer a comprehensive alternative was Henry Clay, whom Kentucky's legislature had elected to the Senate in 1849. Many Whigs fully expected Clay, who had bitterly refused to endorse Taylor's nomination in 1848, to try to rally congressional Whigs against the new administration, just as he had led them against John Tyler. Almost seventy-three when he returned to Washington in December, Clay disdained Taylor as hopelessly unfit for the presidency. And he clearly hoped to rally all congressional Whigs behind his plan, thus reasserting that he, rather than the unqualified soldier in the White House, still commanded the Whig Party. But his proposal did not simply reflect political jealousy. Shocked at the level of sectional asperity he found in Washington, he also considered Taylor's plan inadequate to avert a now-imminent threat of disunion.

On January 29, therefore, Clay presented eight resolutions to the Senate as a blueprint for how Congress might resolve the deepening sectional crisis. In brief remarks on January 29 and a much fuller speech a few days later, he specifically referred to his plan as a comprehensive "compromise" that would settle all matters involving slavery then in dispute. He also declared that he was asking Northerners to make greater concessions than Southerners because slaveholders had much more at stake.

The content of Clay's resolutions (and they were simply proposals for how the Senate should proceed rather than specific pieces of legislation) belied this assertion. Clearly aware that northern Whigs vastly outnumbered southern Whigs in the House, Clay primarily aimed his proposals at winning those Northerners' backing. He did ask Congress to pass a new fugitive slave bill, and by the time he spoke, the Senate's judiciary committee had already reported out a new law offered by the Virginia Democrat James M. Mason. He also called on Congress to pass resolutions, not laws, stating that it was "inexpedient" for it to prohibit the interstate slave trade or to abolish slavery in the District of Columbia, both of which Free-Soilers demanded. At the same time he urged Congress to abolish the public slave auctions in the District, as Northerners had long sought. His recommendations for the Mexican Cession, however, most glaringly demonstrated his pro-northern tilt.

Just like Taylor, Clay called on Congress to admit California as a free state when its constitution finally arrived. But he explicitly insisted that Congress create territorial governments in the remainder of the Cession without waiting for a state constitution from New Mexico. He wanted no "restriction or condition, on the subject of Slavery" in those territorial bills because, Clay insisted, "Slavery does not exist by law, and [because of the arid climate] is not likely to be introduced into any of the Territory acquired by the United States from the Republic of Mexico." Here Clay was indeed asking northern Whigs to abandon the proviso; but as he made emphatically clear in his accompanying speeches, Northerners did not need Wilmot's proviso to stop slavery extension. Mexico's antislavery statutes had continuing legal force in the Cession, and they would prohibit it in the absence of any explicit congressional "restriction or condition, on the subject of Slavery."

Unlike Taylor, Clay also sought to settle the Texas–New Mexico boundary dispute and on terms far more congenial to northern Whigs than Polk had posited. Obviously aware of the odd configuration of New Mexico on Polk's 1848 map, Clay proposed to run the boundary separating Texas from New Mexico directly eastward along the thirty-second parallel from El Paso on the Rio Grande to the Sabine River, which divided Louisiana from Texas. Everything south of that line would become the new state of Texas. Everything north of it, including Dallas, Fort Worth, and some twenty thousand slaves, would be given to New Mexico, from which, Clay had just insisted, slavery was barred by Mexico's antislavery statutes. In return for this concession by Texas, Clay asked Congress to appropriate an unspecified sum of money to pay off Texas's bonded debt. Because the holders of the depreciated Texas bonds, almost all of whom were Northerners or Europeans, would receive this federal payment rather than the state of Texas, Clay was effectively recommending stripping Texas of half the area it claimed for no monetary compensation whatsoever.

Clay later boasted that his "whole system of measures, as originally proposed" on January 29, subsequently passed Congress to become the Compromise of 1850, and some historians have mistakenly repeated that preposterous assertion. As soon as Clay sat down on January 29, in fact, nine southern senators—eight Democrats and one Whig—jumped to their feet to protest that his supposed "compromise" was outrageously unjust to the South. They denounced California's admission as a free state and demanded instead extension of the Missouri Compromise line to the Pacific coast. They flayed Clay for stating that it was merely "inexpedient," rather than flatly unconstitutional, for Congress to abolish the interstate slave trade and slavery in the District of Columbia. They condemned his proposed Texas–New Mexico boundary for what it was: a direct assault on slavery and the South because it hugely reduced the area in which slavery was legal and from which additional slave states might be carved. And they homed in on the linchpin of Clay's proposal for organizing territorial governments without the proviso, ostensibly his biggest concession to the South on the territorial question. Prohibition of slavery extension by Mexican law, they shouted, was just as intolerable as prohibition by the proviso. No Southerner could ever acquiesce to that atrocity. Congress must explicitly replace Mexico's antislavery statutes with laws fairer to slaveholders' rights.

This attack was so forceful and cogent that no southern Whigs dared support Clay's plan any more than they dared support Taylor's. Nor would northern Whigs embrace Clay. Despite its concessions, his plan entailed the political suicide of organizing territorial governments without the proviso. "Henry Clay's Compromise Bill will not satisfy Whigs in this region," chorused Whigs across the North. "The territories had better be left to form states according to President Taylor's plan." Clay's "whole system of measures, as originally proposed," in short, did not become the Compromise of 1850. Instead, it ignited a tumultuous, exhausting, and agonizing eight-month struggle in Congress to shape a more acceptable, or at least passable, compromise than the plan Clay had offered.

Northern Democrats in the Senate quickly reshaped Clay's proposals into a Democratic compromise, even though Clay retained nominal leadership of the pro-compromise forces. Douglas, as chairman of the Senate's Committee on Territories, wrote and introduced bills that admitted California as a free state and organized the New Mexico and Utah Territories on a popular sovereignty basis. His bills, that is, granted territorial legislatures the right to decide on slavery and thus replace Mexico's antislavery statutes if they wished. Douglas's Democratic allies in the House introduced identical bills, and in both chambers most southern Whigs and most northern Democrats rallied behind them. They continued to do so even when Southerners later amended those territorial bills with language that explicitly required future Congresses to admit any states formed from those territories with or without slavery as their state constitutions prescribed at the time of admission. Because this language prohibited future Congresses from denying admission to new slave states, it was a decidedly pro-slavery "condition" absent from Clay's original proposals.

Both Clay and Douglas wanted Congress to act on these bills individually, but from February on Mississippi Democrat Henry Foote insisted that the Senate form a special select committee that would consider all matters regarding slavery, including the District slave trade and fugitive-slave bills, together. Fearful that Northerners, especially in the House, might admit California and then, as Taylor had asked, do nothing else, Foote obviously wanted to bundle all matters regarding the Mexican Cession into a single bill. That way Northerners would have to accept territorial governments without the proviso as the price of California's admission. In April, Foote finally prevailed, and the Senate appointed a select committee chaired by Clay. On May 8, it reported three bills: Mason's fugitive-slave act, which had been ready for Senate action since early January; a bill abolishing public slave auctions, but not slavery itself, in the District of Columbia; and an "omnibus" bill that contained all the measures for the Mexican Cession, including a new Texas–New Mexico boundary proposal that restored much, but not all, of the land to Texas that Clay had earlier proposed stripping from it.

The location of the Texas–New Mexico boundary was in fact Foote's chief concern in pushing for a select committee. Both before and after its formation, debates and roll-call votes on that question consumed most of the Senate's time. Like almost all other southern Democrats, Foote insisted that Texas retain every acre of soil east of the Rio Grande because any reduction of Texas would shrink the area where slavery was already legal and from which additional slave states might be carved. Foote wanted a select committee primarily as a means to pressure border-state Whigs, who had never accepted Texas's grandiose boundary claims, to join southern Democrats in permanently fixing Texas's western boundary at the Rio Grande. Unless those Whigs did so, Democrats like Foote warned, they would bury the new fugitive-slave bill, in which border states had the greatest stake. Northern Whigs protested against this demand, but the senator who most stridently opposed Foote on the issue and insisted on moving the boundary hundreds of miles to the east of the Rio Grande was Missouri's Benton, who had been trying to reduce the size of Texas since 1844. The debates between Benton and Foote grew so furious, indeed, that at one point, when Foote feared that the powerful Benton was going to attack him physically, Foote drew a pistol and threatened to shoot Benton.

Bundling the boundary settlement with all other measures for the Cession in a single bill made the Texas–New Mexico issue the pivot that decided if a compromise could pass. Southern Democrats found Clay's new boundary proposal of May 8 no more satisfactory than his earlier one. In contrast, Benton and northern Whigs believed that it still gave Texas, where slavery was legal, too much land at the expense of New Mexico, where it was not. Any Southerner who accepted any reduction of Texas could be accused of betraying his section; any Northerner who acquiesced in either New Mexico's organization on a popular sovereignty basis or Texas's claim to the Rio Grande could be accused of betraying his.

Events during the summer only increased the importance of the boundary issue, but the public's attention, and that of many subsequent historians, was captured instead by three Senate speeches in March that had little to do with it. On March 4, South Carolina's mortally ill Calhoun listened as Virginia's Mason read his final speech to the Senate. Once again rehearsing a long series of supposed northern violations of southern equality and threats to slavery, Calhoun announced flatly that Southerners must secede if California gained admission as a free state.

Three days later Daniel Webster delivered what instantly became famous (or infamous) as his "Seventh of March" speech. "I wish to speak today, not as a Massachusetts man, not as a northern man, but as an American," he began. "I speak today for the preservation of the Union. Hear me for my cause." Webster advocated compromise, but not specifically Clay's compromise. He did not endorse the creation of territorial governments, but if they were organized, he said, the North should forgo imposition of the proviso since climate alone would prevent slaveholders from entering those territories. Nor did he offer a proposal for the Texas–New Mexico boundary, but he did remind Northerners that they were bound by the terms of Texas's annexation to admit up to four more slave states from it. What made this speech particularly obnoxious to most northern Whigs, however, was that he passionately insisted that Southerners deserved a more effective fugitive-slave law. Webster "has ruined himself politically," chorused furious Whigs across the North when they read newspaper accounts of his speech. "He's as dead as a herring." He had done nothing to persuade most northern Whigs to abandon Taylor's plan.

Four days later, on March 11, New York's freshman Whig Senator William H. Seward, the leader of antislavery northern Whigs in Congress, flayed legislative compromises as "radically wrong and essentially vicious." He demanded California's immediate admission, "directly, without conditions, without qualifications, and without compromise." He would oppose anything that allowed slavery extension into the Mexican Cession, including Texas's claim to the Rio Grande boundary, since the Constitution devoted the national domain "to union, to justice, to defence, to welfare, and to liberty." Indeed, there was "a higher law than the Constitution, which regulates our authority over the domain, and devotes it to the same noble purposes." The Cession was part of God's creation for the good of all people. "We are his stewards, and must so discharge our trust to secure . . . their happiness." Congressmen, not natural causes such as an arid climate, must exclude slavery from the Cession. It was their duty as God's "stewards."

Seward's speech infuriated Southerners from both parties and intensified their opposition to Taylor's plan. Nor were Seward and other northern Whigs able to prevent the creation of the select committee that presented the omnibus bill on May 8, exactly the kind of compromise Seward disdained. Until the end of July, however, northern Whigs captained by Seward, Delaware's two Whig senators, and southern Democrats stopped southern Whigs and northern Democrats from passing the omnibus.

While Congress was stalemated, three events in June and July ultimately broke that stalemate. The Nashville Convention, called by Mississippi the previous November, met as scheduled in June. But once it seemed likely that Congress might pass a satisfactory compromise, southern Whigs refused to send delegates, and a few slave states were entirely unrepresented. A smattering of genuine secessionists attended, but they went unheeded. Instead, the convention endorsed southern Democrats' call for extending the Missouri Compromise line to the Pacific coast with slavery explicitly legalized south of it. It also called for the delegates to reassemble after Congress adjourned to assess what it had done. This anticlimactic fizzle only encouraged opposition to the omnibus by southern Democrats, who saw their stance identified as the South's, and by northern Whigs, who saw the anticlimax as evidence that no serious secession threat requiring compromise in fact existed in the South.

Developments farther west were much more ominous. During the spring, Governor Peter H. Bell of Texas attempted to solidify his state's claim to everything east of the Rio Grande by formally establishing Texas counties on the eastern bank of that river. His agent started at El Paso, and then worked his way northward toward Santa Fe, but when he reached that town, the U.S. military commander insisted he desist because Santa Fe was the property of the United States, not Texas. When the agent reported this rebuff to Bell in June, the furious governor called for a special session of the Texas legislature to meet in mid-August to authorize an expedition of Texas militia to seize Santa Fe by military force from the U.S. troops then occupying it. Bell also sent a letter to Taylor demanding to know if he had ordered the actions of his commander at Santa Fe. In short, if the anticlimax at Nashville reduced the chances of immediate secession, developments in Texas raised the chances of a shooting civil war between a slave state and the national government.

Word of these developments reached the East weeks before Bell's official letter of protest did. The reaction was alarming indeed. Across Dixie, Southerners pledged to send volunteers to aid Texas in any military confrontation with federal troops. Furious Southerners in Congress demanded that Taylor explain what his orders to Santa Fe had been. In a reply to Congress on June 17, 1850, Taylor thrilled most northern Whigs by insisting that all the areas where Texas had tried to organize new counties belonged to the United States, not to the state of Texas. Those areas would remain in the possession of the United States "until the question of boundary shall have been determined by some competent authority. Meanwhile, I think there is no reason for seriously apprehending that Texas will practically interfere with the possessions of the United States."

In fact, however, rumors instantly circulated in Washington that Taylor planned to reinforce the army detachment in Santa Fe and even to take the field himself in order to prevent Texas from seizing Santa Fe. These rumors proved to be the final straw for southern Whigs. For over a year they had boiled with resentment at Taylor's patronage appointments in their home states. Then, in mid-May, the administration's newspaper in Washington attacked Clay for egotistically seeking credit for resolving the crisis and declared in no uncertain terms that Taylor would stand by his own plan, which he considered infinitely superior to the omnibus. To southern Whigs, Taylor's obstinacy posed the biggest obstacle to passing a compromise, for northern Whigs would stick to their guns as long as he stuck to his. And now he seemed intent on provoking a shooting war at Santa Fe. Frantic southern Whigs sent emissaries to the White House in early July to demand that Taylor clarify his intentions. Exactly what was said in those interviews is unknown, but when Alexander Stephens emerged from the White House, he vowed to launch impeachment proceedings against Taylor if he sent reinforcements to Santa Fe.

On July 4, only days after Stephens issued this threat, Taylor spent hours in the hot sun at a ceremony near the construction site of the Washington Monument. Returning to the White House, he consumed huge quantities of iced milk and fruit. That night he took sick, probably from acute gastroenteritis. Whatever the cause, he declined rapidly even as southern Whigs were pillorying his stand on Santa Fe in the House. On the night of July 9, Taylor died. No event was more important in securing passage of the Compromise of 1850.

Vice President Millard Fillmore succeeded Taylor as President. A New York Whig, he had been added to the ticket in 1848 to mollify the northern Whig regulars incensed by Taylor's nomination. Since Taylor's inauguration, Fillmore had been ruthlessly excluded from the inner workings of the administration, and to his deep embarrassment his archrival within New York's Whig Party, Seward, had won the lion's share of federal patronage in New York at the expense of his own allies. Nonetheless, since December 1849, he and his closest New York friends had staunchly defended Taylor's plan for the Cession. On July 10, the day of his swearing in as President, Fillmore demanded the resignations of everyone in Taylor's reviled cabinet, but no one knew where he now stood on the congressional compromise.

Within days of assuming office, Fillmore discovered Governor Bell's angry letter about Santa Fe and his threat of calling out Texas militia in mid-August to seize it. This discovery immediately converted Fillmore to the pro-compromise camp, for only a quick congressional settlement seemed likely to avert bloodletting at Santa Fe. Thus he appointed only sectional moderates to his new cabinet. The most important of these was Daniel Webster, his Secretary of State, who was now firmly committed to passage of a congressional compromise. During the last two weeks of July the new administration exerted all the pressure it could on northern Whigs to abandon their opposition to the omnibus and allow its passage, if only by abstaining rather than voting against it.

That pressure was formidable. By late July the Senate had still taken no action on most patronage appointees Taylor had nominated, and hundreds of other names had not yet even been sent to the Senate. Fillmore could replace all of these men with new ones. He and especially Webster made it abundantly clear to northern Whigs in the House and Senate that their friends would be replaced and their enemies appointed unless they abandoned their resistance to the compromise. Simultaneously, northern Democratic senators like Dickinson, Cass, and Sturgeon told northern Whig senators and representatives that how they reported on patronage nominees depended on how those Whigs voted on the omnibus bill.

Neither appeals to patriotism nor intimidation, however, could save the omnibus bill from derailment. On July 31, the Senate eviscerated it. The occasion was an amendment from a Maryland Whig outraged by a Democratic proposal about how, finally, to redraw the Texas–New Mexico boundary that clearly advantaged Texas's claims. The accumulated anger among Whigs from both sections about the terms of Texas annexation in 1844 and Polk's insistence that the Rio Grande was Texas's western boundary now exacted its price. As a result, anti-compromise senators deleted everything related to Texas, New Mexico, and California from the omnibus, leaving the Utah territorial bill as its only surviving passenger.

Importantly, the pattern of votes on the roll calls that upended the omnibus was the same as that on earlier and later votes in the Senate and then in the House on the compromise. Northern Democrats and southern Whigs strove to keep the omnibus, and thus congressional compromise, intact. The two Free-Soil senators, all northern Whigs except Pennsylvania's James Cooper (who wanted the Democrat Sturgeon's help on Pennsylvania patronage decisions), and southern Democrats voted to kill it. And when they did so, they literally danced jigs in the aisles.

Anti-compromise men celebrated prematurely. Later that same night the Senate passed the Utah territorial bill despite the opposition of most northern Whigs. Without the price of California's admission, southern Democrats could support a measure whose popular sovereignty provisions opened up the possibility, however remote, of slavery's extension into that area. Despairing that chances of compromise were now finished, the physically exhausted Clay left Washington to recuperate at Newport, Rhode Island. Now the Democrat Douglas, the forceful "Little Giant" who had always opposed the bundling strategy, managed the bills.

Douglas was confident that he could pass all the bills individually through the Senate, and he wanted to take up California statehood first. At this point, Fillmore's administration made its most decisive contribution to passage of the Compromise of 1850. On August 6, Fillmore officially informed Congress of the Texas threat to march on Santa Fe. Even more firmly than Taylor, he declared Santa Fe and the areas east of the Rio Grande part of New Mexico and thus property of the United States and announced that his oath of office compelled him to use armed force to repel any "trespassers" from Texas who threatened U.S. authority in the area. Simultaneously, he urged Congress to resolve this crisis quickly by fixing a boundary between Texas and New Mexico that was acceptable to Texas. If possible, moreover, Congress should also settle the other disputes involving slavery before it adjourned.

The following day, the same Maryland Whig who had precipitated the breakup of the omnibus introduced a new Texas boundary bill he had drawn up with Douglas's help. This set the boundary at its modern location, which most northern Whigs considered an intolerable extension of slavery. It also called for Texas to be paid $5 million by the United States as compensation for surrendering its claims. An additional $5 million was to be appropriated to pay off the holders of Texas bonds. On August 9, this bill passed the Senate 30–20. The majority included eleven northern Democrats, six southern Democrats, including both Texans, six southern Whigs, and seven northern Whigs, six of whom came from New England and had previously voted against the omnibus at every chance. In addition, the two New Jersey Whigs who had earlier opposed compromise abstained rather than vote against the measure. Had those eight Whigs voted in the negative, the bill would have failed. In the end, only four northern Whigs joined the two Free-Soilers, two southern Whigs, and twelve southern Democrats, who would not accept anything less than the Rio Grande, in the minority.

Unquestionably, northern Whigs who broke from the previous anti-compromise coalition on this vote wanted to avert a conflict at Santa Fe that might start a civil war. Just as unquestionably, however, they also bent before the pressure of Fillmore, Webster, and northern Democratic senators about retaliation on patronage unless they allowed the bill to pass.

Passage of the Texas boundary bill broke the Senate logjam. Within a week, the California statehood bill and the act organizing New Mexico on a popular sovereignty basis were passed. Only after the measures for the Mexican Cession had been enacted did the Senate turn to the other matters. On August 23, it passed the fugitive-slave bill, which had occasioned surprisingly little debate, 27–12. On September 16, the bill abolishing the public slave markets in the District of Columbia sailed through on a vote of 33–19. All of these votes had a sectional cast. A solid bloc of Northerners with a few pro-compromise Southerners supported California and the District slave-trade bill, and Southerners, aided by northern Democrats, passed the New Mexico and fugitive-slave acts. Notably, on these latter two pro-southern measures, an exceptionally large number of northern Whigs, on New Mexico, and Northerners from both parties, on the fugitive-slave bill, abstained. These Northerners detested those laws but refused to vote against them.

With one very significant exception, votes in the House followed a similar pattern. Pro-compromise Democratic leaders, who controlled the House machinery, feared that Northerners, who outnumbered Southerners, would admit California and enact the new Texas–New Mexico boundary, but then refuse to pass the New Mexico and Utah bills because they allowed slavery's possible extension. Thus they combined the Texas boundary and New Mexico Territory measures into a single bill and insisted that the House consider it first. Immediately dubbed "the little omnibus," this measure required Southerners who wanted New Mexico with popular sovereignty to accept the reduction of Texas and Northerners who liked that reduction to accept New Mexico with popular sovereignty. After a series of achingly close votes, this measure passed 107–99 on September 6. The majority contained twenty-two northern Whigs who had sworn never to allow territories without the proviso but who obviously succumbed to pressure from the administration and northern Democratic senators. Had they adhered to their previous commitments, this bill would never have passed, and the fate of the remaining bills sent over from the Senate would have been cast in doubt.

Instead, the other measures passed quickly. California was admitted, 150–56. Utah succeeded much more narrowly, 97–85, and the seventeen northern Whigs who abstained could have killed it had they joined the majority of their colleagues in voting against it. Again the pressure from Fillmore and Webster had telling effect. Given the House's northern majority, the Fugitive Slave Act passed with surprising ease, 109–76, largely because of heavy northern abstentions. Two northern Whigs and twenty-nine northern Democrats were in the majority. Enactment of the District slave-trade measure 124–59 on September 17 completed the House's work.

Fillmore signed the measures as soon as they reached his desk, and he rejoiced that "the long agony is over." He referred both to the end of the longest, most grueling congressional session held since the adoption of the Constitution and to what he hoped was a permanent settlement of the conflict over slavery extension. In his annual messages of December 1850 and 1851, indeed, Fillmore explicitly called the compromise a "final settlement" of disagreements over slavery. Congressional proponents of the compromise also celebrated their achievement as saving the Union and forever resolving disputes over slavery.

There were grounds for such optimism. Passage of the Texas boundary bill with support from both Texas senators averted the feared clash at Santa Fe. Many Whig and Democratic newspapers around the country praised the compromise and the restoration of sectional peace. Businessmen in northeastern cities who had organized bipartisan Union meetings in the summer to show support for the compromise were especially pleased. Measuring public opinion precisely is impossible; nonetheless, substantial evidence suggests that a majority of Americans in both sections happily accepted the compromise as an end to sectional strife. By definition, however, majorities do not include everyone, and significant minorities in both sections loathed provisions of the compromise package.

Of most immediate danger, many Democrats from South Carolina, Georgia, Alabama, and Mississippi considered California's admission as a free state and the reduction of Texas grounds for immediate secession. As soon as California became a state, Georgia's Democratic governor called for a state secession convention to meet in December, with delegates to be elected in November. Mississippi's Democratic governor, John A. Quitman, called his legislature into special session and persuaded it to schedule a secession convention in late 1851, with its delegates to be chosen in September of that year. Secessionists in Alabama and South Carolina awaited the outcome in Georgia and Mississippi before calling their own conventions.

With its convention scheduled a full year before Mississippi's was to meet, Georgia was the crucial state. There pro-compromise Whigs from the black belt, led by Stephens and Toombs, who had worked heroically in the House for compromise since February 1850, and pro-compromise up-country Democratic non-slaveholders, led by Howell Cobb, the Democratic Speaker of the House who had helped facilitate passage of the compromise, formed a Union coalition against a Southern Rights coalition composed primarily of bitter slaveholding Democrats. At the December convention, pro-compromise Union men over-whelmingly outnumbered secessionists 240 to 43. That rout effectively delayed southern secession for ten years.

Nonetheless, the convention made clear in the so-called Georgia Platform that its acquiescence in the compromise was conditional, not absolute. It pledged that Georgia "would abide by it as a permanent adjustment of this sectional controversy" only if it was indeed permanent. Georgia would resist "to a disruption of every tie that binds her to the Union" any new effort in Congress to abolish slavery in the District of Columbia, to bar slavery from Utah and New Mexico, to prevent the admission of new slave states, or to alter or repeal the Fugitive Slave Act. "Upon the faithful execution of the *Fugitive Slave Law* by the proper authorities [that is, Fillmore's administration]," the Georgia Platform concluded, "depends the preservation of our much beloved Union."

The triumphant Union coalition also announced in December that it intended to make the realignment of political forces in Georgia during 1850 permanent by running Union candidates in the state and congressional elections of 1851 against the outnumbered Southern Rights forces. The Union Party easily elected the Democrat Cobb governor the following October, and the new Union majority in the state legislature sent Toombs to the Senate to replace John M. Berrien, one of the few southern Whigs to oppose the compromise in 1850.

Similar realignments occurred in Mississippi and Alabama in 1851. Non-slaveholding Democrats joined with slaveholding Whigs in new Union parties. Running on the Georgia Platform, they routed Southern Rights parties composed primarily of anti-compromise slaveholding Democrats in congressional, gubernatorial, and state legislative elections. The compromise had been affirmed as acceptable to the South, however grudgingly, and secession had been stopped cold (as it was in South Carolina as well). The by-product of that achievement, however, was what turned out to be the permanent destruction of the two-party system of Whigs and Democrats in those three states. Democrats would recover by 1852; Whigs would not.

Elsewhere in Dixie's elections of 1850 and 1851, jousting over the compromise assumed the partisan lines that had emerged in Congress. Democratic candidates denounced the compromise as a sellout of Southern Rights; Whigs defended it as just to the South and necessary for the preservation of the Union. In almost every slave state, moreover, pro-compromise Whigs won the majority of offices at stake, usually because nonslaveholding Democrats who accepted the compromise refused to vote for Democratic candidates who continued to denounce it. Buoyed by those victories, Whigs across the South by the end of 1851 had started to demand that their party nominate Fillmore for President in 1852 so they could retain their advantage on the compromise issue. Indeed, to southern Whigs' delight, Fillmore used every power he possessed, including calling out troops, to enforce the Fugitive Slave Act in the North.

Popular and political reactions to the compromise in the North were the mirror image of those in the South. Whigs in the North suffered greater internal divisions over it than did Democrats. Northern Democrats defended the compromise as necessary to save the Union, whereas the majority of northern Whigs blasted the territorial bills for allowing slavery's possible extension. From Maine to Michigan, Whigs publicly and privately execrated Clay, Webster, and Fillmore for their roles in securing the compromise. They considered its terms a betrayal of everything northern Whigs had stood for on the slavery issue since 1844. Unless northern Whigs repudiated the compromise, most Whig politicos believed, their voters would abandon them for the Free-Soil Party. "We must make war on this administration to save the Whig party from contempt and scorn," wrote one of Seward's New York allies. Ohio Whig Senator Ben Wade was more succinct: "God save us from Whig Vice Presidents."

The territorial provisions were bad enough, but the new Fugitive Slave Act most infuriated Northerners, and not just Whig politicos. While Southerners were making its enforcement the *sine qua non* for their remaining in the Union, Northerners were erupting in ever more organized rage over the terms of this new law. To facilitate the recapture of runaway slaves in the North, the law called for the appointment of new federal commissioners to sit in judgment of accused fugitives. It also provided that U.S. marshals should help slaveholders track the runaways down. Those alleged fugitives were denied the right to testify or to have juries decide their fate. In this star-chamber setting, commissioners were encouraged to discover runaways: for every black they returned to slavery, they received ten dollars; if they declared the accused to be free, they earned five dollars. Nor did the law apply only to instances of hot pursuit. Blacks who had lived as free men and women for years in northern communities might be accused and consigned to slavery. For white Northerners, the worst provision of the law allowed for them to be fined and imprisoned if they aided slaves in escaping or even if they refused to join posses called by marshals in pursuit of fugitives. The law forced white Northerners to become slave catchers themselves, to act at the beck and call of southern slaveholders. In short, they could be symbolically reduced to the status of slaves.

Enactment of the Fugitive Slave Act provoked Harriet Beecher Stowe to write her famous antislavery novel, *Uncle Tom's Cabin*. First published in serialized form in a Free-Soil Party newspaper, it became a runaway best-seller when it appeared as a book in 1852. Some 300,000 copies sold within the first year. Between 1850 and the end of 1852, moreover, northern mobs in a few well-publicized episodes snatched captured fugitives from the authorities and sped them to freedom in Canada. Nonetheless, thorough research by historians reveals that in most instances the new law was peacefully enforced. However much Northerners might revile the law, the vast majority of them believed that it must be obeyed as long as it was the law of the land.

Still, the law was reviled, and most northern Whigs believed they would be slaughtered in the North's congressional and state elections of 1850 and 1851 unless they called for its immediate revision or repeal and were free to criticize other pro-southern parts of the compromise as a betrayal of Whig principles. Those northern Whigs faced opposition from northern Democrats, who proudly trumpeted their role in passing the compromise and blasted its Whig critics for recklessly endangering the Union. In every northern state, moreover, a minority of Whigs remained loyal to the new Fillmore administration, which insisted on the finality of the compromise. Those administration loyalists tenaciously fought against Whig platforms and candidates that refused to accept the compromise as the final word on slavery matters. "The present administration will not recognize one set of Whig principles for the North, and another for the South," Webster insisted as early as October 1, 1850.

The result during 1850 and 1851 was a series of increasingly bruising battles between pro-administration and anti-administration Whigs in the North's district and state party conventions to choose the party's nominees and write its plat-forms. Anti-administration, anti-compromise Whigs usually won those intra-party battles, but then lost elections to pro-compromise Democratic candidates because pro-compromise Whigs refused to vote for them. In response to these setbacks, by the end of 1851 anti-compromise Whigs had become determined to prevent either Fillmore or Webster, who openly sought the office, from getting the party's presidential nomination. Instead, they attempted to secure it for General Winfield Scott, the particular favorite of Seward, Fillmore's archrival.

By the start of 1852, however, northern Whigs had decided to abandon their criticism of the Compromise of 1850. The results of the North's elections of 1850 and 1851, just like those in the South, clearly demonstrated that running against the compromise was a political loser. The majority of people in both sections accepted it. Therefore, both Whig and Democratic politicos decided to woo back their parties' pro-compromise elements who had defected or stayed home in 1850 and 1851. In 1852 both parties wrote national platforms pledged essentially to the finality of the compromise. Democrats, indeed, explicitly pledged that their party would never allow any further discussion of slavery in the halls of Congress.

Not all Whigs or Democrats accepted these endorsements of the compromise. Former Southern Rights Democrats were incensed, and die-hard Southern Rights Democrats actually ran their own presidential candidate that year. Conversely, Horace Greeley, who edited the most widely read Whig newspaper in the North, represented many northern Whigs when he wrote of his party's platform: "We defy it, execrate it, and spit upon it." Nonetheless, by the summer of 1852 the two major parties had officially reached a consensus about the finality of the compromise as a permanent settlement of the slavery extension issue.

That consensus, importantly, destroyed the ability of parties to run Janus-faced campaigns on slavery issues in the different sections.

That inability hurt Whigs far more than Democrats, for Democrats were far more united behind their presidential nominee, Franklin Pierce of New Hampshire, than Whigs were behind their candidate, Winfield Scott. The Whig national convention of 1852 was almost as divided as that of 1848. Together Webster and Fillmore, who allowed his name to be floated for the nomination with great reluctance, controlled a majority of delegates. That's one reason why the convention wrote a pro-compromise platform. With solid backing from the South, Fillmore's supporters far outnumbered Webster's, but Webster refused to release his delegates to Fillmore. As a result, Scott, the favorite of most northern Whigs, ultimately prevailed. But Scott was anathema to many southern Whigs. They viewed him as the hated Seward's man. He had refused to pledge himself publicly to the finality of the compromise prior to the convention, a pledge upon which southern Whigs had insisted for months. As a result, a number of southern Whig congressmen publicly announced that they could not support Scott. It was evident from the moment of his nomination that he would be crushed across the Deep South, as he indeed was.

Whigs thus entered the campaign with glaring disadvantages. They seemed certain to lose the entire Deep South and many other slave states because Scott's commitment to the compromise was suspect. They were bereft of economic issues because the prosperity ignited by the California gold rush and heavy foreign investment in rapidly expanding American railroads had rendered Whig calls for positive governmental promotion of economic growth obsolete. And they could gain no traction on the slavery issue in the North, as they had in 1844 and 1848, because of the national platform's commitment to the finality of the compromise. The upshot was what even Whigs called a "Waterloo" Whig defeat. Scott carried only four states—Vermont, Massachusetts, Kentucky, and Tennessee—and Pierce routed him in the electoral vote 254–42. Whig candidates in congressional and state races ran almost as dismally; and in the next Congress, Democrats would hold a two-thirds majority in the House and an outsized majority in the Senate as well.

Democrats won in 1852 because of dramatic Whig abstention in the South and a huge increase of immigrant votes for Democrats in the North, despite a concerted effort by Whigs that year to win the immigrant vote. More important as far as the slavery extension issue was concerned, the rate of voter participation dropped to 69.6 percent of the potential electorate, the lowest turnout level since 1836. What was most notable about the 1852 campaign, in fact, was the ubiquitous commentary from Whigs, Democrats, and independents, South and North, about the pervasive apathy among the electorate. That apparent indifference to the outcome is understandable. Both parties were committed to the finality of the compromise. Economic prosperity seemingly rendered governmental economic policies irrelevant. And both the Democratic and Whig parties divided internally over new concerns of the public, like the clamor for state-enacted laws prohibiting the manufacture, sale, and consumption of liquor ignited by passage of Maine's prohibition law in 1851. But "state-enacted" is the key phrase here, for while Whigs tried to portray Pierce as a drunkard—"the hero of many a well fought bottle," they jeered—prohibition at that time fell squarely within the jurisdiction of state governments, not Washington. Thus the issue had only tangential importance to a national race.

Slavery extension, in contrast, clearly fell within national jurisdiction; that's why Congress had stalemated on it for four years after the introduction of Wilmot's proviso. One with an inquiring mind might logically ask, with both major parties committed to the finality of the compromise, why that dodge did not benefit openly sectional parties, as both Whigs and Democrats had long feared. The cold fact is that it did not. Georgia's George M. Troup, the separate anti-compromise Southern Rights candidate, barely won 5,000 votes across Dixie, when the national total exceeded 3 million votes. And John P. Hale, the Free-Soil Party's candidate, won only about 157,000 northern votes, compared with Van Buren's 291,000 in 1848. In the North, indeed, both Whigs and Democrats had added new voters since 1848; only the Free-Soilers had lost them.

This decline, like the overall drop in the rate of voter participation, is of immense help in fathoming public opinion in the North at the end of 1852, just as Troup's minuscule showing and Scott's rout in Dixie because of massive Whig abstentions help us understand the South. The drop in the Free-Soil vote raises withering, if not unanswerable, questions about most historians' frequently iterated insistence that *Uncle Tom's Cabin* massively increased animosity toward slavery among northern voters. Antislavery voters had a clear alternative in 1852, the Free-Soil Party, yet even they apparently considered voting for it pointless, since the Compromise of 1850 had permanently settled the slavery extension issue. When the year ended, most Americans expected never to have to confront that divisive question again.

4

THE KANSAS-NEBRASKA ACT

Despite widespread public relief that the Compromise of 1850 had forever buried the vexatious slavery extension issue, its purported "permanent settlement" lasted only three years. In his inaugural address in March 1853, Franklin Pierce announced that, quite unlike his timid Whig predecessors, he intended to seek further territorial acquisitions for the United States. He especially coveted that part of northern Mexico south of the Gila River, and Spain's slaveholding colony Cuba. Pierce kept his targets secret, however. Consequently, during 1853 few cries against additional slave territory rose in the North. Instead of debates over slavery's potential status in future acquisitions, the extension question reemerged in early 1854 over territory where slavery's status had apparently been long fixed—the northern Louisiana Territory, from which slavery had been "forever prohibited" by the Missouri Compromise of 1820. Ironically, the question arose in part because of the earlier feud over the Wilmot Proviso and Democrats' insistence by 1852 that the Compromise of 1850 constituted a final settlement of *all* slavery extension matters.

In 1820 Southerners had given fuller support to the Missouri Compromise package than did Northerners because of the latter's continued opposition to Missouri's admission as a slave state. By the early 1850s their positions on that compromise had switched. Since Missouri's admission in 1821, Iowa, directly north of Missouri, had become a new free state in 1846, and shortly thereafter Congress formally organized the free territory of Minnesota. The remaining land north of the Missouri Compromise line remained unorganized at the end of 1852, but Northerners confidently regarded the pledge that slavery must be excluded from it as sacrosanct.

By then, however, many Southerners had begun to scorn the bargain their predecessors had struck in 1820. Arkansas, directly south of Missouri and thus south of thirty-six degrees thirty minutes, had entered the Union as a slave state in 1836. The only other part of the Louisiana Territory south of that slavery-prohibiting line had been set aside as Indian Territory for tribes forcibly transported from east of the Mississippi River in the 1830s and 1840s. Ironically, Jackson's Indian-removal policy, aimed at gaining more land for white farmers and slaveholding planters in the Southeast, precluded any further western slavery extension in the Louisiana Territory.

That exclusion was not just ironic. In the early 1850s many Deep South Democrats still fumed that California's admission as a free state had upset the precious sectional balance of power in the Senate, even though California's two Democratic senators usually voted with the South. These Southerners knew that Minnesota and Oregon might soon become additional free states. With slavery prohibited from the remainder of the Louisiana Territory, where, they wondered, could new slave states be obtained to offset this growth of northern political power? As some proponents of the Compromise of 1850 had argued to win northern support for it, the popular sovereignty provisions of the Utah and New Mexico bills meant little in practice, for the arid climate prevented slaveholders from rushing to those territories. Some Southerners lusted after Central America or Cuba as sites of additional slave states, but even with Pierce's support the chances of acquiring them were uncertain. Instead, the area that seemed most likely to produce a new slave state was that part of the unorganized Louisiana Territory directly west of Missouri.

In 1850 slaves constituted only 13 percent of Missouri's population and slaveholders barely more than that proportion of its white families. But slaveholders heavily settled the western part of the state, east of the Missouri River. If slavery could flourish there, it might also prosper in the lands adjacent to that river's western bank. In addition, those slaveholders greatly feared that any new free territory organized west of the Missouri might become a sanctuary for their own absconding slaves. Democratic Senator David R. Atchison, long Thomas Hart Benton's chief antagonist in the state Democratic Party, championed these western Missouri slaveholders. As he and his slaveholding supporters fully recognized, preventing the organization of free territory and opening the potential for a new slave state required that the Missouri Compromise's ban on slavery north of thirty-six degrees thirty minutes be eliminated.

By the end of 1852, many southern Democrats outside Missouri had come to consider that long-standing prohibition anathema. Calhoun's Southern Address of 1849 had listed it as Northerners' initial violation of Southerners' equal rights. Six years of denouncing the Wilmot Proviso as outrageously insulting had convinced many other southern Democrats that the 1820 line was just as intolerable, for it, too, constituted congressional prohibition of slavery from western territories. What southern Whigs may have thought at this point was irrelevant, for Democrats thoroughly dominated both houses of Congress. A bill to establish a territorial government with slavery prohibited in part of the unorganized area easily cleared the House of Representatives in the winter of 1852–53. But southern Democrats blocked its passage in the Senate because the Missouri Compromise's ban on slavery remained in place.

The pressure to organize the area west of Missouri and Iowa did not go away, however, and, it must be emphasized, that pressure did *not* come from land-hungry southern slaveholders or even southern politicians hoping to create a new slave state. Instead, it arose from two northern sources. One was farmers seeking cheaper land than they could find in rapidly populated midwestern states. Those farmers could not gain legal title to any land in the Louisiana Territory until Congress formally organized territorial governments. Only then could the federal government survey the land and put it up for sale at government land offices. Since the acquisition of Oregon and California, moreover, numerous proposals had sprouted up to build one or more railroads from the East to the Pacific coast. What route or routes such railroads might take generated considerable dispute, but everyone realized that so ambitious a project required federal subsidies in the form of land grants that railroads could sell to raise construction funds. Any route from the Midwest across the Louisiana Territory, however, required the government to survey land into sections that could be granted to railroads. Proponents of a transcontinental railroad thus joined the cry for formally organizing the area west of Missouri and Iowa. Neither land-hungry farmers nor railroad promoters had any desire to change the 1820 prohibition of slavery extension. They simply wanted territories organized.

In December 1853, at the start of the Thirty-third Congress, with its huge Democratic majorities in both houses, Iowa Democrat Augustus Dodge introduced a bill into the Senate organizing the area west of Missouri and Iowa into the Nebraska Territory. Senators then sent the bill to the Senate Committee on Territories, chaired by Stephen A. Douglas, who had managed passage of the compromise bills through the Senate in 1850.

Douglas had sought formal organization of this area since he first arrived in Congress in 1844. An ardent nationalist, he hoped to build up the West's population so it could act as a balance wheel between the North and the South. Douglas also desired construction of a transcontinental railroad, especially if its eastern terminus were in Chicago or Superior City, Wisconsin, where he had extensive landholdings whose value stood to increase handsomely if the Pacific railroad originated in either city. Douglas astutely recognized the obstacles. He had written friends as early as November 1852 that no territory could ever be organized unless Congress somehow bypassed the prohibition of slavery extension; southern Democrats in the Senate simply would not allow it. Throughout 1853 both northern and southern Democratic newspapers called for organizing the area on the popular sovereignty basis of the Compromise of 1850, and when Congress opened in December 1853, Douglas privately promised an Illinois lieutenant that he would write a Nebraska bill which did precisely that. As it soon became clear, his rationale for doing so, a flagrantly dishonest rationale indeed, was that Congress in 1850 had meant the popular sovereignty provisions of the compromise to apply to all federal territories and not simply to Utah and New Mexico.

By the end of 1853 a number of other Democrats had reached a similar conclusion, if for reasons different from Douglas's. The framing of what became the Kansas–Nebraska Act of

1854 in fact repeated and adumbrated all of the fateful connections between politicians and slavery extension that had appeared since the emergence of the Texas annexation question in 1843. Politicians made decisions from short-term calculations of partisan, factional, or personal advantage rather than from any long-term concern for the health, indeed, the very preservation, of the Union. Unlike earlier instances in the 1840s, grassroots popular pressure at the end of 1853 existed to formally organize territorial governments in the remainder of the Louisiana Territory. But, once again, politicians, not the public at large, made the fateful decisions regarding slavery's expansion into those territories—decisions that this time ultimately propelled the nation into civil war.

After his inauguration in March 1853, Franklin Pierce had attempted to unite the Democratic Party by distributing his cabinet seats and lesser federal patronage appointments to all elements of the party, both to those who had supported and to those who had opposed the Compromise of 1850. This effort incensed Democrats everywhere, but especially those who had supported the compromise most faithfully, former members of Union coalitions in the Deep South and northern Democrats who had fought tooth and nail against coalitions of Free-Soilers and Democrats. Feuds over which Democrats got federal plums were ubiquitous, but intra-party conflict in New York engendered explosive ramifications for the entire nation.

The straightforward rivalry of the 1840s among New York Democrats, which pitted conservative Hunkers against Van Buren's Barnburners, had evolved by the early 1850s into a three-way struggle, the Hunkers having divided over readmitting the Barnburners into the Democratic fold after 1848. So-called Hardshell Hunkers intensely opposed giving Barnburners any public offices, whether elective or appointive. Softshell Hunkers welcomed the Barnburners back with open arms. And the Barnburners themselves only grudgingly accepted the popular sovereignty provisions of the Compromise of 1850 that the Hards' leader, ex-Senator Daniel S. Dickinson, had done so much to enact. Pierce tried to straddle this division by giving patronage plums to prominent men from all three groups, but this evenhanded stance infuriated the Hards. In 1853 Hards ran their own state ticket against the Soft-Barnburner nominees. The Democratic split allowed New York's Whigs to win the election, one of only two victories northern Whigs enjoyed that year. In retaliation, Pierce replaced the most prominent Hard patronage holder in New York with a Soft. In response, Hards publicly vowed to secure Senate rejection of the Soft and Barnburner appointees when they came before the Senate for confirmation in 1854 unless those men toed Hards' line on party policy.

Because the Democratic national platform of 1852 had pledged the party to the Compromise of 1850 as a final settlement of all slavery issues, the Hards sought a test that might secure Senate rejection of Soft and Barnburner appointees. They insisted that the Democratic Party now maintained that the popular sovereignty provisions of the compromise applied to all federal territories, including Louisiana. If those nominees rejected that interpretation in written or oral testimony to Senate committees, as Hards fully expected, they would be denied confirmation. If they dared to accept it, their constituents, especially among the Barnburners, would repudiate them. In short, Hards intended to revive the slavery extension issue simply to use it as a weapon in an intra-party power play involving northern Democrats.

For this hardball strategy to work, of course, New York's Hards needed help from Senate Democrats, especially southern

Democrats. This help materialized, for southern Democrats had already rejected any organization of a new territory west of Missouri and Iowa if slavery were banned from it according to the Missouri Compromise. Of particular importance here were four Senate Democrats who, because they roomed together in the same boardinghouse on F Street in Washington, were known as the F Street Mess: Andrew Pickens Butler of South Carolina, an acolyte of the deceased Calhoun; Virginia's Robert M. T. Hunter and James M. Mason, author of the Fugitive Slave Act and another Calhoun disciple; and Missouri's David R. Atchison. Chairmen of the Senate's four most important committees, these Southerners seethed over Pierce's appointments of one-time Free-Soilers and their sympathizers to federal jobs in the North. Thus they readily agreed with Hards that a new, more pro-slavery test of Democratic orthodoxy must be passed before they would confirm such men. Once the Nebraska bill was consigned to Douglas's Committee on Territories, therefore, Atchison informed Douglas that he, his messmates, and indeed all southern Democrats would never support a Nebraska territorial bill that included the eternal prohibition of slavery written into the Missouri Compromise.

Douglas had recognized their looming opposition as early as November 1852. By the end of 1853, however, he had also been flooded with warnings that discontent at Pierce's patronage allotment would wreck the Democratic Party unless Pierce or the Democratic majority in Congress struck on a policy initiative that was bold enough to rally all Democrats behind it. As a Pennsylvania Democrat worried by his party's widely publicized internal feuds had written Pierce's Attorney General, Democratic disarray could be ended only by a specific policy "that will raise invective from the other side and compel us to quit our domestic quarrels." Here was the classic rationale for a two-party system, one that Van Buren had articulated to Thomas Ritchie as early as 1827. The best way to unite one's own party was to provoke opposition from its rival. Pierce, however, had no domestic policy initiatives that would serve the purpose; his still-secret initiatives for foreign expansion constituted his only policy.

Thus Douglas decided to fill that void and save the Democratic Party from disintegration by reinstigating conflict with Whigs over a program for western development. His program was three-pronged: construction of a transcontinental railroad with federal land grants; a homestead law giving away free land in the West to attract settlers; and formal territorial organization of the area west of Iowa and Missouri, on which the other parts of his plan depended. On January 4, 1854, Douglas reported out from his committee a bill organizing the Nebraska Territory. This bill, he wrote an Illinois ally, "will form the test of Parties, & the only alternative is either to stand with the Democracy or to rally under [the Whig William H.] Seward." The good of the Democratic Party, not of the nation, was Douglas's top priority. As a Louisville, Kentucky, newspaper editor later assessed Douglas's reasons for introducing the bill, "The politician constructed a new arena for party gladiators at the expense of the repose and temper of the nation."

To pass this party-salvaging bill, as Atchison had made clear, Douglas needed the support of southern Democrats, who would no longer tolerate retention of the Missouri Compromise's declaration that slavery must be "forever prohibited" from Nebraska. Douglas fully understood that outright repeal of that prohibition would infuriate Northerners, who by 1854 had come to consider it sacred. Thus he sought to make an end run around it, in part because he sincerely believed that slavery would never be extended to the new territory. His January 4 bill copied language directly from the Utah and New Mexico measures of 1850, stating that "when admitted as a State or States, the said Territory, or any portion of the same, shall be received into the Union with or without slavery, as their constitutions may prescribe at the time of their admission." It further declared that territorial legislatures would have authority over all rightful subjects of legislation, presumably including slavery. Douglas accompanied this bill with a committee report that specifically recommended *against* either "affirming or repealing the 8th section of the Missouri act," that is, the Missouri Compromise line.

Northern Whigs in the Senate like Seward immediately wrote friends that Douglas had gone as far toward repeal of the ban on slavery extension as he dared. Southern Democrats did not see it that way. In their reading of Douglas's bill, the Missouri Compromise line would still prohibit slaveholders from entering the new territory until it was ready to apply for statehood. If so, slavery extension was impossible since Northerners would write antislavery state constitutions. They immediately told Douglas his bill did not suffice. On January 10, Douglas reported a twenty-first section of the bill that had allegedly been omitted from the first version by clerical error. This section specified that "all questions pertaining to slavery in the Territories, and in the new states to be formed therefrom are to be left to the people residing therein, through their appropriate representatives." Here was the classic northern Democratic definition of popular sovereignty: elected territorial legislatures should make the decision on slavery extension.

Nonetheless, Whigs and Democrats spotted a loophole. The Missouri Compromise ban might still apply until the territorial legislature was elected, in which case no slaveholders would sit in the legislature that decided on slavery extension. In the House, an Alabama Democrat quickly proposed a bill flatly repealing the Missouri Compromise line. In the Senate, Kentucky Whig Archibald Dixon announced on January 16 that as soon as the Senate's legislative agenda allowed, he would move an amendment to Douglas's bill repealing the line. This announcement threw southern Democrats into a tizzy, for they refused to let southern Whigs outflank them on the slavery issue. Meanwhile, Hunker Democrats wanted an even higher hurdle for Barnburner appointees to clear in order to gain Senate confirmation. Both groups renewed pressure on Douglas for further changes. He made them, and over the weekend he secured a pledge from President Pierce to endorse the measure as a new test of Democratic Party orthodoxy.

Douglas presented this version, which would subsequently undergo slight revision, on Monday, January 23, 1854. The new bill created two territories, not just one: Kansas, immediately west of Missouri, and Nebraska, west of Iowa and running northward to the boundary with Canada. Whatever the reason for this decision, it gave the impression to outraged Northerners that a deal had been cut. Kansas was to be given to slaveholders while Nebraska would remain free soil. Douglas still blanched at explicitly repealing the Missouri Compromise line. Instead, his new bill declared that the Missouri prohibition had been "superceded by the principles" of the Compromise of 1850 and was therefore "inoperative and void." As if this language were not sufficiently clear, two weeks later Douglas added two further explanatory clauses. One stated that "the true intent and meaning of this act [is] not to legislate slavery into any Territory or State, nor exclude it therefrom, but to leave the people thereof perfectly free to form and regulate their domestic institutions in their own way, subject only to the Constitution of the United States." The other now declared that the Missouri restriction was "inoperative and void" because it was "inconsistent with the principle of non-intervention by Congress with slavery in the States and Territories" as recognized by the "compromise measures" of 1850. In short, in response to southern pressure, Douglas had changed the justification for popular sovereignty from northern Democrats' stress on territorial legislatures' decision-making power to southern Democrats' stress on nonaction by Congress with regard to slavery extension.

Dixon's threatened amendment clearly precipitated these changes, and that Dixon was a Whig shows once again how the slavery extension issue could become a political football to be exploited by politicians for personal or partisan advantage, regardless of the consequences to the nation as a whole. Many years later, in fact, Seward claimed that he, of all people, persuaded Dixon to threaten his repeal amendment on January 16. However astonishing this claim seems at first blush, there was a political logic to it if true. Because they lacked compelling issues to take to the electorate, Whigs in both sections had been in a tailspin since their rout in 1852. Douglas's bill opened the chance for them to again run Janus-faced campaigns on the slavery issue. Just as Tennessee Whig Milton Brown's amendment to the Texas annexation resolution had given southern Whigs a chance to pose as stauncher defenders of slaveholders than southern Democrats, so Dixon's proposed amendment might give badly needed ammunition to southern Whigs in 1854 and 1855. They could claim responsibility for repealing the Missouri prohibition and again opening chances for slavery to expand. Conversely, by making the Nebraska bill even more obnoxious to Northerners than it already was, the amendment would allow northern Whigs to campaign in 1854 by pillorying the Democratic bill as an outrageous Slave Power aggression aimed at spreading slavery farther and keeping white Northerners out of the West.

No contemporary evidence from 1854 exists to corroborate

Seward's later claim, however, and at that time he explained Douglas's revision as a result of pressure from Hardshell Hunkers who wanted a bill Barnburners could never support. Nor is there any evidence that most southern Whigs sought this supposed trump card in January 1854. Dixon, in fact, had selfish personal reasons for threatening the amendment. Within weeks, the Kentucky legislature would decide whether to return him to the Senate, and he was wooing Democratic, not Whig, support for his reelection. But because Dixon in fact never moved his amendment, Douglas's bill as it stood on January 23 was indelibly a Democratic measure. On that day most Whigs, including many Southerners, had good reasons to oppose it.

Antislavery Whigs across the North, as well as in Congress, erupted in anger as soon as Douglas presented his first bill on January 4. Even its terms subverted the eternal prohibition of slavery north of the Missouri Compromise line, and they found the subsequent revisions still more outrageous. That Douglas justified his bill as being inherent in the popular sovereignty provisions of the Compromise of 1850 vindicated their earlier opposition to that measure. It also increased their contempt for the conservative Fillmore loyalists who had insisted on the finality language in the 1852 Whig platform. But embarrassed pro-compromise Whigs from the North who had promised that the compromise was a permanent settlement of the slavery extension question were equally outraged by the bill. They knew that it, far more than Harriet Beecher Stowe's novel, would revive antislavery political forces in the North, thereby aiding their factional Whig rivals like Seward and betraying "the promise of that cessation of agitation which the Compromise of 1850 held out." As supporters of the compromise, moreover, they were especially infuriated by Douglas's rationale. "Clay & Webster could have and would have, blown this bill to atoms," fumed one. "Overthrowing the Compromise of 1820," echoed another northern Whig, was "the last thing which either Mr. Clay or Mr. Webster would have assented to."

To stave off a renewal of sectional polarization that could only help their intra-party rivals and endanger the very preservation of the Union, conservative Whigs hoped to frame the party's opposition to the bill in partisan rather than sectional terms. Instead of portraying it as a Slave Power aggression against the North, as Seward and his allies clearly intended, they wanted to paint it as an unforgivable violation of the Democratic Party's platform pledge in 1852 never to allow another matter involving slavery to enter the halls of Congress. Democrats, after all, controlled the White House and outnumbered Whigs 37 to 22 in the Senate and 159 to 71 in the House. They wrote the bill, they revised it, and they were responsible for it. For this tack to succeed, however, conservative northern Whigs desperately needed the few southern Whigs remaining in Congress to join them in opposing the bill. Whigs clearly lacked the votes to stop it, unless popular protests in the North forced northern Democrats in the House to oppose it. But if Whigs united as a party against it, their chances of flaying it as a Democratic Party, rather than a southern pro-slavery, measure in subsequent elections would be greatly enhanced.

As of January 23, 1854, in fact, northern Whigs had several reasons to expect that most of their southern Whig colleagues might join them in opposing Douglas's bill. For one thing, despite Douglas's last-minute linguistic alterations, his provision for a decision by territorial legislatures had long been reviled in the South as "squatter sovereignty," since it allowed the earliest (and presumably scrubbiest) settlers to make the decision on slavery. Thus southern Whigs had political cover for opposing the bill. Far more important, southern Whigs inside and outside

Congress strongly doubted that slavery could ever be established in Kansas or Nebraska. Hence there was absolutely no pressure on southern Whig congressmen from their constituents to support the bill. All that the South would gain from Douglas's measure, protested Tennessee's Whig Senator John Bell, was an "abortive abstraction," while its passage was bound to reawaken antislavery agitation in the North and probably disrupt the Whig Party along sectional lines. Whig papers from New Orleans, Louisville, Raleigh, Savannah, and elsewhere denounced the measure as Democratic demagoguery and reminded southern Whig congressmen that they were pledged by their party's 1852 platform to oppose any revival of the slavery question.

On Tuesday, January 24, the day after Douglas presented his revised bill, however, the chances that southern Whigs would rally with their northern colleagues against it evaporated. On that day, the few remaining Free-Soilers in Congress—Senators Charles Sumner of Massachusetts and Salmon Chase of Ohio, along with four members of the House—published the "Appeal of the Independent Democrats in Congress to the People of the United States." This manifesto lacerated Douglas's bill as "a gross violation of a sacred pledge," as "part and parcel of an atrocious plot" to spread slavery and exclude northern whites from the new territories, and as a "bold scheme against American liberty" that would subjugate the entire nation "to the yoke of a slaveholding despotism." "Shall a plot against humanity and democracy so monstrous, and so dangerous to the interests of liberty throughout the world, be permitted to succeed?" Not if they could help it. If the bill became law, they vowed to "go home to our constituents, erect anew the standard of freedom, and call on the people to . . . rescue . . . the country from the dominion of slavery."

The sincerity of these sentiments is unquestionable. None-theless, it is just as certain that the Free-Soilers also sought to exploit Douglas's measure for their own partisan purposes. Since mid-1852 the northern public, aside from genuine abolitionists, who had always been and remained a tiny fraction of the North's white male electorate, had been unconcerned about slavery and uninterested in the Free-Soil Party. In the North's state elections of 1853, indeed, Free-Soilers had dropped the slavery issue altogether and campaigned as foes of liquor consumption or proponents of state constitutional reform in order to keep the party alive. To perpetuate their party and their own political careers, Free-Soilers needed something new to arouse antislavery anger in the North. Douglas had given it to them—and in spades.

The Free-Soil "Appeal" preempted the grounds for opposition to the bill. From a conservative Whig condemnation of a Democratic measure that violated sectional peace, it switched to a sectional attack on an act of aggression by the Slave Power against the North. By identifying opposition with men Southerners regarded as abolitionists, it also made it almost impossible for any southern Whig to oppose the measure. "It is unfortunate that the free soil senators have been suffered to lead off the opposition," complained one of Fillmore's conservative Whig allies from Washington. "This fact more than anything else has contributed to unite southern sentiment on the bill." A year later, when surveying the political wreckage wrought by the Kansas-Nebraska Act, the exceedingly conservative Massachusetts Whig Robert C. Winthrop was still protesting that the Free-Soilers had "usurped a lead which belonged to others, and gave an odor of abolition to the whole movement." Now southern honor was at stake, and just as all Southerners had to oppose

Wilmot's proviso, so they now had to support the Nebraska measure.

At a hastily called caucus of southern Whig senators on February 15, all but Tennessee's Bell pledged to vote for Douglas's bill, and on March 4, when it easily passed the Senate 37 to 14, nine southern Whigs joined the majority. Only Bell sided with its opponents, although Delaware's Clayton, who missed the vote, later announced that he also would have voted against it. Even had those ten southern Whigs supported the opposition, the bill would still have passed the Senate. In the House, with its large northern majority, however, southern Whig support proved crucial.

Representatives were always more directly susceptible to public pressure than senators, who were chosen by state legislatures for six-year terms. Since January, a storm of protest had erupted across the North against the repeal of the Missouri Compromise line. All of the reasons that had prompted northern support for the Wilmot Proviso powered this anger, but two additional factors increased it. While Northerners had little interest in distant places like Utah and New Mexico, many of them hoped to move to the areas contiguous to Missouri and Iowa and feared they would be prevented from doing so if slaveholders also went there. But even for Northerners with no wanderlust, the repeal of a thirty-four-year-old pledge against slavery extension into that area was intolerable. Many northern Democrats wavered before this popular wrath. When the Nebraska bill passed the House on May 22 by a vote of 113 to 100, northern Democrats split precisely in half—forty-four in favor and forty-four against. Southern Whigs, in contrast, divided thirteen in favor, seven against, and four not voting. Had those southern Whigs united in opposition, as their northern colleagues implored them to do, the bill would have failed in the House. Instead, Pierce signed the Kansas–Nebraska Act into law on May 30, 1854.

Because of its results, the Kansas–Nebraska Act is arguably the most consequential piece of legislation ever passed by the U.S. Congress. Those results relating to slavery's possible extension into Kansas (no one expected slaveholders to move to Nebraska) took a while to develop, but the political fallout was instantaneous and proved enduring. For one thing, northern outrage scotched Pierce's ambitious plans for territorial expansion. The treaty with Mexico acquiring the Gadsden Purchase south of the Gila River almost lost in the Senate in the spring of 1854 because Northerners feared additional slavery expansion into it. It finally succeeded only after senators significantly reduced the size of the acquisition James Gadsden had negotiated. The larger lesson was clear: any prospect that Congress would now allow annexation of slaveholding Cuba was doomed.

So was the northern wing of the Democratic Party. As some perceptive northern Democrats instantly feared, their party suffered a terrific backlash from furious northern voters determined to punish it for sponsoring the Kansas–Nebraska Act. This realignment of the North's electorate against Democrats lasted until the congressional elections of 1874 and even longer in presidential contests. The dimensions of this anti-Democratic landslide can be measured in several ways. In the Congress that passed the Kansas–Nebraska Act, northern Democrats held ninety-one seats in the House; in the North's congressional elections of 1854 and 1855, they lost sixty-six of those seats. Of the forty-four northern Democrats who voted for the Kansas–Nebraska Act, only seven won reelection. Viewed somewhat differently, in the three-way presidential contest of 1852, Franklin Pierce won almost 50 percent of the North's popular vote;

in 1856, in another three-man race, Democratic candidate James Buchanan garnered a little more than 41 percent of the region's vote. That was a huge swing; indeed, one of the main reasons that the Republican Abraham Lincoln won the presidency in 1860 is that by 1856 Democrats had already been reduced to a minority of the northern electorate.

If the backlash against the Kansas-Nebraska Act devastated Democrats politically, however, it, in combination with other crucial factors, also contributed to the final destruction of the Whig Party. Southern Whig support for Douglas's measure in Congress disrupted the party along sectional lines. Unlike the previous sectional divisions over the Wilmot Proviso and the Compromise of 1850, this breach proved irreparable. From January 1854 on, northern Whigs both inside and outside Congress, antislavery Sewardites and conservative pro-compromise Whigs alike, warned that southern Whig support for a measure that opened up the West to slavery extension would "be a finishing blow to the Whig party" since northern Whigs could and would never cooperate with southern Whigs again. "No man has struggled as I have to preserve it as a national party," accurately protested Connecticut's Whig Senator Truman Smith, who since 1842 had served as the de facto national chairman of the party. But "I shall have nothing to do with any Southern Whig who joins Stephen A. Douglas in introducing into Congress & into the country another controversy on the subject of slavery."

Southern Whig votes for the bill were thus proclaimed to be "the ultimate disruption and *denationalization* of the Whig party." The "break" with southern Whigs was "final," Truman Smith vowed in late May. "I hope to hear no more of national parties," snarled Ohio's Whig Ben Wade. "Never was a greater mistake made than in passing the Nebraska bill," moaned the disconsolate conservative Winthrop in June 1854. He saw "nothing ahead but discord & deviltry."

Northern Whigs' fury at what they regarded as southern Whigs' betrayal instantly caused Free-Soilers to implore them to leave the Whig Party and join them in a broad new northern antislavery party built around opposition to the Kansas-Nebraska Act and slavery extension. A May editorial in Free-Soilers' leading newspaper called upon the people of the North "to disregard obsolete issues, old prejudices, mere party names, and rally as one man for the re-establishment of liberty and the overthrow of the Slave Power." In 1854 this appeal met with limited success. In four midwestern states where the Whig Party had already been weakened by significant voter losses since 1850—Ohio, Indiana, Michigan, and Wisconsin—broad anti-Nebraska or "People's" coalitions consisting of indignant Whigs, Democrats, and Free-Soilers quickly emerged after the act's passage in May to challenge its offending Democratic authors. In Michigan and Wisconsin, those coalitions labeled themselves the Republican Party as early as the summer of 1854. The creation of the Republican Party, in short, directly resulted from the Kansas-Nebraska Act.

The initial state platform of Michigan's Republicans well encapsulated the purpose and thrust of the new organization. After denouncing the institution of slavery as "a relic of barbarism," calling for renewed defiance of the Fugitive Slave Act, and insisting that Congress prohibit slavery extension to check the "unequal representation" of the South in Washington, it declared that the purpose of the Kansas-Nebraska Act was to "give the Slave States such a decided and practical preponderance in all measures of government as shall reduce the North . . . to the mere province of a few slaveholding oligarchs of the South—to a condition too shameful to be contemplated." Thus the platform ringingly concluded: "That in view of the necessity of battling for the first principles of republican government, and against the schemes of aristocracy the most revolting and oppressive with which the earth was ever cursed, or man debased, we will co-operate and be known as Republicans until the contest be terminated."

Over time this Republican call for Northerners to unite in a defensive sectional phalanx against Slave Power aggressions would gain much greater salience among Northerners, but in 1854 most northern Whigs outside the four states already mentioned wanted no part of a new party or a coalition with Free-Soilers. The reason was clear. Every northern Whig in the House and Senate had voted against the Kansas-Nebraska Act, and many northern Whigs and Democrats expected Whigs to sweep the North's congressional elections and indeed the presidential election of 1856 by running against it. The party had ruptured along sectional lines, but as one Pennsylvania Whig wrote in May 1854, "The Whig party of the North is, this day, stronger than at any former period." New York's Seward was especially adamant in spurning Free-Soilers' advances and insisting that the northern Whig Party was the only antislavery party Northerners needed. So, too, was Illinois's Abraham Lincoln, a devoted Whig since the party's formation in 1834 who, while running as a Whig for the state legislature in 1854, explicitly rejected appeals from Free-Soilers to join a new Republican Party.

Lincoln did not demand the immediate abolition of slavery, but his anger at the prospect of slavery extension opened by the Kansas-Nebraska Act abruptly ended his self-imposed retirement from active political participation. Convinced that slavery was a "monstrous injustice" and intolerably immoral, Lincoln also believed that the nation's Founders had never expected it to survive as long as it had. He saw its possible future extension as wantonly prolonging a violation of the heroic Founders' intentions to create a republic devoted to liberty. In a memorable speech at Peoria, Illinois, on October 16, 1854, he made clear that his concern was the *extension* of slavery, not its *existence* in southern slave states. But the constitutionality of slavery in those states furnished no excuse for its extension into free territory in violation of the Founders' expectations. Douglas's callous overthrow of the Missouri Compromise threatened the very preservation and perpetuation of "the blessings of our glorious Union" that its passage in 1820 had secured.

Lincoln won election to the Illinois state legislature as an anti-Nebraska Whig in 1854, although his adherence to the Whig Party prevented his election by that legislature to a U.S. Senate seat in 1855. Elsewhere, many northern Whigs triumphed in 1854 by denouncing slavery extension and the Kansas-Nebraska Act. The absolutely critical facts, however, are that those victorious Whig candidates did not win solely because they opposed slavery extension and that many Whigs who trumpeted their opposition to slavery extension lost. Usually they did not lose to pro-Nebraska Democrats. Instead, they were defeated by yet another new party that arose in the political turmoil which erupted between 1853 and 1856, a party whose existence had little to do with African-American slavery or its possible extension.

This was the American or Know-Nothing Party, an anti-Catholic, anti-immigrant, and antipolitical incumbent organization that began to emerge in 1852 and 1853, well before the introduction of Douglas's bill. Appalled by the economic, social, and political evils that had supposedly accompanied the massive European immigration to the United States since 1846 and by the eagerness of both Whigs and Democrats to solicit Catholic and immigrant votes, Know-Nothings vowed to proscribe all Catholics and all foreigners from public office, to change naturalization laws so that recent immigrants could not vote, and to elect only candidates "fresh from the ranks of the people" rather than the spoils-hungry hacks now leading the Whig and Democratic parties. Very specific developments in the early 1850s intensified native-born Protestants' fear of and animosity toward Catholic immigrants and entrenched politicos. The point here is that those antagonisms fueled a grassroots political revolt in 1854 and 1855 that threatened to eclipse any concern about the Kansas-Nebraska Act or slavery extension among northern—and southern—voters.

In the North in 1854, most victorious Whig candidates for state offices or Congress had Know-Nothing backing, and that was also true of anti-Nebraska or Republican coalitions in Ohio, Indiana, and Michigan. Where those anti-Nebraska Whig candidates did not have such backing, they often lost despite intense northern outrage at the possibility of slavery extension. As one New York Whig wrote after his state's 1854 contests, "This election has demonstrated that, by a majority, Roman Catholicism is feared more than American slavery." In northern elections during 1855, moreover, Know-Nothing candidates almost always bested candidates of the new Republican Party, even if Democrats prevailed because the anti-Democratic opposition divided its favors. And in the South, where an antislavery, anti–southern party like the Republicans' had no chance of flourishing, the Know-Nothings had supplanted Whigs as the Democrats' major opponents by the end of 1855.

The point cannot be emphasized enough. The reemergence of the slavery extension issue caused by passage of the Kansas-Nebraska Act in May 1854 infuriated the northern public and spawned the creation of the exclusively northern and overtly anti-southern, antislavery Republican Party. It also decisively contributed to the wreck of the Democratic Party's electoral

fortunes in the North. Yet antiforeign and anti-Catholic sentiment was just as important in causing Democratic defeats in 1854
and 1855, just as it was indisputably more important than
antislavery or free-soil sentiment in killing off the Whig Party
in the North. Northern Whigs tried to exploit the North's
deep anger at the Kansas-Nebraska Act in 1854 and 1855, but that
effort failed to deter Know-Nothing incursions into their electorate. Only after the extent of northern Whig losses to Know-
Nothings in the 1854 elections became clear, indeed, did Whigs
like Seward and Lincoln, both of whom abhorred the bigotry of
Know-Nothings, finally abandon their old party and join the
Republicans. Simultaneously, the 1854 elections in the North
convinced most southern Whigs that they must abandon the
Whig Party and become Know-Nothings themselves if they had
any hope of defeating Democrats. In short, Know-Nothingism,
and the passionate anti-Catholic, anti-immigrant, anti-politician
resentments it expressed, were equally if not more important
than the Kansas-Nebraska Act in destroying the Whig Party.

By the start of 1856, in fact, most political observers were
predicting that the Know-Nothings, not the emerging Republican Party, would elect the next President. Yet by the end of 1856,
the Republicans, rather than the Know-Nothings, had replaced
the Whigs as Democrats' primary political opponent. They did
so largely because of what had happened with regard to slavery
extension on the ground in Kansas since passage of the Kansas-
Nebraska Act in May 1854. The Republican Party had emerged
because of northern outrage at a specific event—passage of the
Kansas-Nebraska Act. For the party to grow, it needed further
evidence of Slave Power aggressions against the North. Subsequent events in, or about, Kansas provided that evidence.

Most of the settlers who moved into Kansas once land went
on sale were small farmers from the Midwest and non-

slaveholders from the upper South, including some Missourians. Most had little interest in the slavery extension question and shared a common desire to keep all blacks, free or slave, out of Kansas. Like all frontiers, Kansas also attracted a number of men hoping to make a quick buck from land speculation, and these included the federally appointed governor, Andrew H. Reeder. Nonetheless, some slaveholders hoping to create a new slave state did appear in Kansas along with their chattels, as did some New Englanders whose primary goal was to stop slavery extension by controlling the new government. Of vast importance, almost all Northerners moving to Kansas did so by traveling up the Missouri River from St. Louis, a route that carried them through the heart of slaveholding country in western Missouri. Regarding these northern settlers as an invasion of abolitionists, those Missouri slaveholders redoubled their determination to legalize slavery in Kansas.

Egged on by ex-Senator Atchison, whose term ended in early March 1855, hundreds of heavily armed Missourians, aiming to exploit an ambiguity in the original act as to what constituted "residency" in Kansas, poured across the border when Kansas's first territorial legislature was elected on March 30, 1855. These "Border Ruffians" took over polling places in sparsely populated hamlets and cast not only their own ballots but hundreds of additional, wholly fictitious ballots for pro-slavery legislative candidates. This fraud yielded a heavy majority of pro-slavery men in the new legislature, and they immediately passed draconian pro-slavery laws. To hold office in the territory, including its legislature, one had to swear an oath that slavery was and would forever remain legal in Kansas. Harboring a fugitive slave was punishable with ten years at hard labor, and circulating abolitionist literature became a capital offense. In response to these laws, men elected by Northerners resigned from the new territorial legislature in a huff and helped set up a rival "free-state" government of Kansas in the town of Lawrence, a government that the Democrat Pierce's administration denounced as an outlaw regime.

With Northerners and Southerners in Kansas pledging allegiance to rival territorial governments, clashes between the two sides were inevitable. The worst of these was the bloody mass murder of five southern, and presumably pro-slavery but non-slaveholding, settlers along Pottawatomie Creek by the abolitionist fanatic John Brown and his sons in late May 1856. The most widely publicized of them, however, occurred days earlier on May 21, 1856. Then a posse that included hundreds of Missourians invaded Lawrence, destroyed the printing presses of the "free-state" newspaper, and burned some buildings. No one was killed, but the Republican press in the East immediately labeled the "Sack of Lawrence" as the start of a war in Kansas over slavery in which "Freedom" was "Bloodily Subdued." "Bleeding Kansas" thus became a powerful weapon in the Republicans' propaganda arsenal during the 1856 presidential campaign, for the Democratic administration clearly sided with the pro-slavery forces.

Republicans gained an even more potent weapon from an event that occurred in Washington simultaneously with the "Sack of Lawrence." On May 19 and 20, 1856, Republican Senator Charles Sumner of Massachusetts, a former Free-Soiler who hated slavery and slaveholders, harangued the Senate with a carefully rehearsed speech called "The Crime against Kansas." In it he denounced the violations of popular sovereignty by Missouri's Border Ruffians and the suppression of northern settlers' basic civil liberties by the pro-slavery Kansas legislature. What most appalled Southerners and other senators, however, was his vicious verbal assault on South Carolina and its senior senator, Andrew Pickens Butler, who was absent from the capital. In retaliation for these insults, on May 22 South Carolina Representative Preston S. Brooks, Butler's cousin, accosted Sumner at his desk on the Senate floor and beat him into bloody unconsciousness with a gutta-percha cane.

The caning of Sumner electrified the North and drove most northern Know-Nothings into the arms of the Republican Party. The party nominated John C. Frémont for President in June on a platform that denounced slavery as "a relic of barbarism," demanded that Congress prohibit it from all federal territories, and rehearsed at length a litany of Slave Power outrages against Northerners in Kansas. "Bleeding Kansas" and "Bleeding Sumner" gave Republicans a nearly invincible combination of issues in 1856. That combination was the political legacy of the Kansas-Nebraska Act. As a result, Republicans carried eleven of sixteen free states that year and 45 percent of the North's popular vote, compared with the Democrat James Buchanan's 41 percent. The Know-Nothings' presidential candidate, Millard Fillmore, captured the remaining 14 percent. Though running last, Fillmore attracted sufficient votes in the crucial lower North states of Illinois, Indiana, and Pennsylvania to give them and the election to Buchanan. Nonetheless, by the end of 1856 the new Republican Party, itself a product of the Kansas-Nebraska Act, had emerged as Democrats' primary opponent in American political life. Know-Nothings' earlier predominance proved ephemeral.

Between 1856 and 1860 the Republicans attracted almost all of Fillmore's 395,000 northern voters as well as the great majority of northern votes cast by young men entering the electorate after 1856. And they did so in large part because of further events growing out of the slavery extension question. Within days of Buchanan's inauguration in March 1857, the Supreme Court delivered its notorious *Dred Scott* decision. Scott was a

Missouri slave who had lived for some years with his owner in Illinois and then in what became the Minnesota Territory. Upon his return to Missouri, he sued in the state's courts for his freedom on the grounds that having lived so long in areas that prohibited slavery, he was no longer a slave. Missouri's courts rejected this plea, and Scott was then sold to a new owner who lived in New York. The U.S. Constitution specifies that legal disputes between citizens of different states are to be heard in federal courts. Thus Scott now sought his freedom in federal courts as a citizen of Missouri suing his new owner, a citizen of New York. In an intricate decision supported by six justices, five of whom were Southerners, including Chief Justice Roger B. Taney, the Court ruled that Scott was still a slave; that as a black and a slave he had no standing as a citizen to sue in federal courts; and, most important, that the Missouri Compromise's prohibition of slavery north of thirty-six degrees thirty minutes, on which Scott based his claim to freedom, was unconstitutional since it deprived slaveholders of their property rights without due process of law, in violation of the Fifth Amendment.

Congress itself, of course, had already repealed that prohibition three years earlier, but the *Dred Scott* decision infuriated Republicans because it held that their platform's central plank—congressional prohibition of slavery from the territories—was unconstitutional. Republicans refused to accept the legitimacy of that ruling, and instead they denounced the decision by a Court dominated by Southerners and Democrats as further evidence of a Slave Power conspiracy. The decision also challenged Douglas's cherished popular sovereignty doctrine, for, slaveholders immediately asked, if Congress could not constitutionally bar slavery from territories, how could it delegate that authority to territorial legislatures? Douglas's instant answer, one that he maintained through the presidential election of 1860, was that territorial legislatures need not positively prohibit slavery to prevent its spread. They could simply refuse to pass the positive laws necessary to sustain slavery in any area, laws criminalizing the theft of slaves from their owners, for example. Without such positive pro-slavery legislation, he insisted, slavery could not expand into the territories.

However clever Douglas's answer, developments in Kansas provided a greater challenge to popular sovereignty, and gave more potent ammunition to Republicans, than did the Supreme Court's decision. Determined to strip Republicans of the "Bleeding Kansas" issue, Buchanan sought to have Kansas admitted as a state, with or without slavery, as soon as possible. He persuaded former Mississippi Democratic senator Robert J. Walker, who had led the Democratic call for Texas annexation in early 1844, to serve as the territory's new governor. Walker agreed, but only after he extracted an explicit promise from Buchanan that any state constitution written by Kansans must be submitted in its entirety to a vote of ratification by all the bona fide residents of Kansas.

Even before Walker reached Kansas, its pro-slavery territorial legislature had called for a constitutional convention to meet in Lecompton in September 1857. Walker tried to persuade the free-state men to participate in the June election of delegates to that convention. But viewing it as thoroughly tainted by pro-slavery influences, they refused. Only some two thousand out of twenty-four thousand potential voters went to the polls in June. As a result, the convention was thoroughly dominated by pro-slavery men. They waited to act, however, until they saw the results of a separate election for a new territorial legislature scheduled for October. Once again, Border Ruffians poured across from Missouri to stuff ballot boxes, but this time the new governor, Walker, threw out fraudulent returns. Consequently, northern settlers for the first time won control of the official legislature of the Kansas Territory.

Infuriated by Walker's interference in the legislative elections, the pro-slavery men who controlled the Lecompton constitutional convention refused to adhere to popular sovereignty. Instead of submitting the entire constitution to a popular referendum, they wrote a document that permanently legalized all slaves, and their descendants, then in Kansas, and gave voters a choice only of accepting the constitution with a provision for the admission of additional slaves or one prohibiting further slave admissions to Kansas. The constitution itself and the legality of the existing slaves in Kansas could not be rejected. Free-state men again boycotted the referendum called by the Lecompton convention, leaving some six thousand pro-slavery men to vote for the constitution with additional slavery. The free-state men now in control of the territorial legislature, however, then called their own referendum on the entire Lecompton Constitution. With pro-slavery elements boycotting the second referendum, some ten thousand votes were cast against the Lecompton Constitution.

Despite this evidence that a clear majority of Kansas's residents opposed slavery and statehood under the Lecompton Constitution, when Congress convened in December 1857, Buchanan insisted that it admit Kansas as a slave state. Douglas instantly broke with Buchanan, denounced the Lecompton document as a palpable violation of popular sovereignty, and joined Republicans in trying to prevent Kansas statehood under it. Here personal conviction was coupled with political calculation, for Douglas realized that northern Democrats would be crushed by Republicans in subsequent elections if Kansas became a slave state over the objections of the majority of its residents. Nonetheless, a Kansas statehood bill easily passed the Senate. In the House, however, northern anti-Lecompton Democrats and Republicans together had enough votes to stop it. The stalemate was broken when a House-Senate conference adopted a bill offered by Indiana Democratic Congressman William H. English. The English bill called for yet another referendum on the Lecompton Constitution in Kansas, ostensibly to approve a reduction in the amount of federally owned land that would be given to the new state. On August 2, 1858, the Lecompton Constitution was overwhelmingly defeated. Kansas would not be a slave state. In 1860 only two slaves still resided within its borders.

The fight over the Lecompton Constitution bitterly divided the Democratic Party. In the North's congressional elections of 1858, anti-Lecompton and pro-Lecompton Democratic candidates often opposed each other, allowing Republicans to capture the seats. For their part, southern Democrats fumed that Douglas had joined Republicans to cheat them out of a new slave state. In the next session of Congress they stripped Douglas of his committee chairmanship and began to demand that Congress establish a federal slave code for the territories if territorial legislatures refused to do so, as Douglas repeatedly declared they could in order to prevent slavery extension. Southern Democrats insisted on such a provision in the party's 1860 national platform. Together with their vehement opposition to Douglas's nomination for President, which most northern delegates supported, this demand disrupted the party's April national convention at Charleston, South Carolina. Ultimately Democrats ran two presidential candidates in 1860: Douglas, supported by most Northerners, and John C. Breckinridge, supported by most Southerners. Most historians agree, however, that even if Democrats had united behind a single man, they could not have stopped Lincoln's election that year.

Despite these developments, in 1858 and 1859 the Lecompton fight proved a two-edged sword for Republicans. On the one hand, by initially discrediting the ability of popular sovereignty to stop slavery extension and, further, by dividing Democrats, it contributed to Republican gains in the 1858 elections, most notably in the three key northern states Buchanan had carried in 1856—Illinois, Indiana, and Pennsylvania. In addition, Buchanan's open endorsement of a new slave state (like Douglas's responsibility for repealing the Missouri Compromise line, Pierce's support for Kansas's pro-slavery territorial legislature, and the Democrat Roger B. Taney's *Dred Scott* decision outlawing congressional prohibition) vastly enhanced the Republican case that Northerners needed an exclusively northern party to stop slavery extension and protect them from Slave Power aggressions. Indeed, in his famous "House Divided" speech of 1858, Lincoln would link these four men together as evidence of a Democratic conspiracy to extend slavery throughout the country that could only be checked by electing Republicans.

On the other hand, the August 2, 1858, referendum in Kansas ended any realistic possibility of slavery extension into any of the existing territories of the United States. That fact seemed to undercut the entire rationale for a Republican Party. Together with Douglas's furious fight against Lecompton, it encouraged former southern Whigs, Northerners who had supported Fillmore in 1856, some anti-Lecompton Democrats, and conservative Republicans to try to displace the Republican Party with a new, bisectional anti-Democratic party that would downplay the slavery issue. Outraged and frightened by this initiative, Republicans responded in various ways to reemphasize the continuing need for an exclusively northern and overtly anti-southern, anti-slavery-extension party.

The Republican national committee issued a circular to justify the party's perpetuation. "The republican party had its origin in the obvious necessity for resistance to the aggressions of the slave power," it declared. Some of the problems forcing its creation had been solved since 1856, "but the attitude of the slave power is persistently insolent and aggressive." Now the Slave Power demanded a federal slave code in the territories and the reopening of the African slave trade. "Upon no organization, except the republican party, can the country rely for successful resistance to these monstrous propositions, and for the correction of the gross abuses which have characterized the present national administration."

In a famous speech at Rochester, New York, in October 1858, Seward sounded similar alarms. Condemning southern attempts to pervert "a republican constitution [into] an aristocratic one," he proclaimed that an "irrepressible conflict" existed between slavery and free labor and that the United States would become "either an entirely slaveholding nation, or entirely a free-labor nation." Slaveholders, he charged, meant to spread slavery not just to the West but to the northern free states as well. "The designs of the slaveholders can and must be defeated," declared Seward, and there was only one way to do so. "The Democratic party must be permanently dislodged from the Government," because the Democratic Party "is identical with the Slave Power." Sectional conflict over slavery extension, in short, was inseparable from partisan conflict between Republicans and Democrats. To defeat the South, Northerners must elect Republicans. Irrefutably correct on the facts, this analysis illustrates once again how politicians readily exploited the slavery extension issue for partisan purposes.

Even more famous to Americans today is the tack that Lincoln took in his now-legendary campaign against Douglas for Illinois's Senate seat in 1858. The legislature, rather than voters at large, chose U.S. senators, but at their state convention in the summer of 1858 Illinois Republicans proclaimed Lincoln as their candidate to replace Douglas in the Senate if Republicans won that fall's state legislative elections. In his speech accepting that nomination, Lincoln told the Republican convention that "a house divided against itself cannot stand" and that "this government cannot endure, permanently half *slave* and half *free*." He did not expect the nation to rupture. Instead, "either the *opponents* of slavery, will arrest the further spread of it, and place it where the public mind shall rest in the belief that it is in course of ultimate extinction; or its *advocates* will push it forward, till it shall become alike lawful in *all* the States, *old* as well as *new*— *North* as well as *South*." As he had said in 1854 and would prove again in the secession winter of 1860–61, Lincoln was concerned far more about the *extension* of slavery beyond the existing slave states than about its *existence* within them.

Lincoln made clear in this speech and his subsequent debates with Douglas that those advocates of slavery included Douglas, Pierce, Buchanan, and Taney, who were softening up the North to accept another Supreme Court decision that would legalize slavery throughout the North. That, he iterated and reiterated, was what was so invidious about Douglas's popular sovereignty doctrine, which Douglas had fought to defend when he joined Republicans' battle against the Lecompton Constitution. Douglas was morally neutral about slavery. He and Democrats like him did not care whether residents of a territory accepted or rejected slavery, as long as those residents had a fair vote. Republicans, in contrast, "*do care* for the result." Republicans believed that slavery was deeply immoral and that the entire nation, not just residents of a territory, had a fundamental stake in whether slavery expanded. To allow that heinous institution any chance to spread—whether by popular sovereignty, a federal slave code, as southern Democrats would soon insist on, or a decision by pro-slavery Democratic judges on the Supreme Court—was to betray the legacy of the nation's Founders who dedicated the United States to freedom, not slavery.

Here we see why Lincoln adamantly opposed any Republican compromise on the slavery extension issue in the secession winter of 1860–61, even as he accepted the proposed thirteenth amendment to the Constitution that winter. Moral principle and faithfulness to the nation's Founders were at stake. Yet precisely because Republicans invested so much more importance in this matter of principle than in the perpetuation of slavery where it already existed, southern Democrats in Congress that secession winter insisted that Republicans make a concession of principle on slavery's extension, not just in the existing Southwest but also in future territories in Central and South America some Southerners hoped to acquire.

Here we see why the nation foundered and split apart on the issue of slavery extension that politicians—some deeply principled, some shortsighted, and some simply selfish—had done so much to shape between 1844 and 1858. Northerners and Southerners rushed to arms in the spring of 1861, after Lincoln called up troops in response to the firing on Fort Sumter on April 12, because of long-accumulated mistrust, fear, and loathing for each other. But these reciprocal popular hatreds did not spring out of whole cloth. Nor were they simply products of the undeniable differences between the social systems of the North and the South and the contrasting value systems those different societies spawned. Rather, they had intensified in response to a series of political decisions and actions in Washington regarding slavery extension and other matters involving slavery. The Civil War was not exclusively a politicians' war. Far too many young Americans fought and died during it for that claim ever to be made. Nonetheless, how politicians in Washington and elsewhere had dealt with the question of slavery extension since the mid-1840s played an undeniable role in causing the bloody conflagration that erupted in 1861 and in which so many Americans gave their lives. What politicians did during those decades had crucial consequences. Their decisions today still do. The fate of their, and, more important, our, nation is still at stake.

APPENDIX: PRIMARY DOCUMENTS

SUGGESTIONS FOR FURTHER READING

INDEX

APPENDIX: PRIMARY DOCUMENTS

LEWIS CASS'S LETTER TO ALFRED O. P. NICHOLSON,
DECEMBER 24, 1847

Michigan's Democratic Senator Lewis Cass, an aspirant for his party's presidential nomination in 1848, addressed this public letter to Alfred O. P. Nicholson, an important Tennessee Democratic leader, in order to announce to the nation his opposition to the Wilmot Proviso and support for popular sovereignty as the best solution for slavery extension. Although he stressed the Union-saving reasons for his position, he was also seeking southern Democratic support for his nomination while simultaneously assuring Northerners that slavery would not expand even without adopting the proviso.

"The Wilmot Proviso has been before the country some time. It has been repeatedly discussed in Congress, and by the public press. I am strongly impressed with the opinion that a great change has been going on in the public mind upon this subject—in my own as in others; and that doubts are resolving themselves into convictions, that the principle it involves should be kept out of the national Legislature, and left to the people of the confederacy in their respective local governments . . .

"Of all the questions that can agitate us, those which are merely sectional in their character are the most dangerous, and the most to be deprecated. The warning voice of him who from his character and services and virtue had the best right to warn us, proclaimed to his countrymen in his farewell address . . . how much we had to apprehend from measures peculiarly affecting geographical portions of our country. The grave circumstances in which we are now placed, make those words of safety; for I am satisfied, from all I have seen and heard here, that a successful attempt to ingraft the principles of the Wilmot proviso upon the legislation of this government, and to apply them to new territory, should new territory be acquired, would seriously affect our tranquility. I do not suffer myself to foresee or foretell the consequences that would ensue, for I trust and believe there is good sense and good feeling enough in the country to avoid them, by avoiding all occasions which might lead to them.

"Briefly, then, I am opposed to the exercise of any jurisdiction by Congress over this matter, and I am in favor of leaving to the people of any territory which may be hereafter acquired, the right to regulate it for themselves under the general principles of the Constitution . . .

"I say this in the event of the extension of slavery over any new acquisition. But can it go there? This may well be doubted. All the descriptions which reach us of the condition of the Californias and of New Mexico . . . unite in representing those countries as . . . generally unfit for the production of the great staples which can alone render slave labor valuable. If we are not grossly deceived . . . the inhabitants of those regions, whether they depend upon their plows or their herds, can not be slaveholders . . ."

PRESIDENT ZACHARY TAYLOR'S
ANNUAL MESSAGE TO CONGRESS,
DECEMBER 4, 1849

In this extract from his annual message, President Zachary Taylor publicly presented for the first time his plan to admit California and New Mexico as states in order to avert further sectional conflict in Congress over the Wilmot Proviso, indirectly alluded to here as one of several "exciting topics of a sectional character which have hitherto produced painful apprehensions in the public mind." Note as well that Taylor implicitly urges Congress to accept the new state constitutions whether or not they prohibit slavery because they were intended by residents "to effect their safety and happiness." Note, finally, that Taylor, like Cass in his Nicholson letter, explicitly invokes George Washington's warning against sectional parties—that is, the Free-Soilers.

"No civil government having been provided by Congress for California, the people of that Territory, impelled by the necessities of their political condition, recently met in convention for the purposes of forming a constitution and State government, which the latest advices give me reason to suppose has been accomplished; and it is believed they will shortly apply for the admission of California into the Union as a sovereign State. Should such be the case, and should their constitution be conformable to the requisitions of the Constitution of the United States, I recommend their application to the favorable consideration of Congress. The people of New Mexico will also, it is believed, at no very distant period present themselves for admission into the Union. Preparatory to the admission of California and New Mexico the people of each will have instituted for themselves a republican form of government, 'laying its foundation in such principles and organizing its powers in such form as to them shall seem most likely to effect their safety and happiness.' By awaiting their action all causes of uneasiness may be avoided and confidence and kind feeling preserved. With a view of maintaining the harmony and tranquility so dear to all, we should abstain from the introduction of those exciting topics of a sectional character which have hitherto produced painful apprehensions in the public mind; and I repeat the solemn warning of the first and most illustrious of my predecessors against furnishing 'any ground for characterizing parties by geographical discrimination.'"

HENRY CLAY'S COMPROMISE RESOLUTIONS
OF JANUARY 29, 1850

Below is the precise text of the original compromise proposals that the Kentucky Whig Henry Clay presented to the Senate as an alternative to Taylor's plan for the Mexican Cession. Note that just like Taylor, Clay strove to persuade Northerners to eschew any attempt to impose the Wilmot Proviso on the Cession, but that unlike Taylor he also called for the Senate to enact a new fugitive-slave law and to eradicate the public slave trade in the District of Columbia. Although Clay later boasted that these resolutions, as originally proposed, were passed as the Compromise of 1850, southern senators immediately denounced them as unfair to the South on January 29, and they were substantially modified, primarily by Democrats, before compromise legislation finally passed in August and September 1850. Nonetheless, note that a close comparison of these resolutions with Cass's Nicholson letter clearly indicates why Clay and Cass ultimately became allies in the pro-compromise camp in 1850.

"It being desirable, for the peace, concord and harmony of the Union of these States, to settle and adjust amicably all existing questions of controversy between them, growing out of the institution of slavery, upon a fair, equitable and just basis: Therefore

"1st. Resolved that California, with suitable boundaries, ought upon her application to be admitted as one of the States of the Union, without the imposition by Congress of any restrictions in respect to the exclusion or introduction of Slavery within those boundaries.

"2. Resolved that as Slavery does not exist by law, and is not likely to be introduced into any of the Territory acquired by the United States from the Republic of Mexico, it is inexpedient for Congress to provide by law either for its introduction into or exclusion from any part of said Territory, and that appropriate Territorial Governments ought to be established by Congress in all of the said territory, not assigned in the boundaries of the proposed State of California, without the adoption of any restriction or condition, on the subject of Slavery.

"3. Resolved that the Western boundary of the State of Texas ought to be fixed on the Rio del Norte [Rio Grande], commencing one maritime league from its mouth, and running up that river to the Southern line of New Mexico, thence with that line Eastwardly, and so continuing in the same direction to the line as established between the U.S. and Spain, excluding any portion of New Mexico, whether lying on the East or the West of that River.

"4th. Resolved that it be proposed to the State of Texas that the United States will provide for the payment of all that portion of the legitimate and bona fide public debt of that State, contracted prior to its annexation to the United States, and for which the duties on Foreign imports were pledged by the said State to its creditor, not exceeding the sum of $_____ in consideration of the said duties so pledged having been no longer applicable to that object, after the said annexation, but having thenceforward become payable to the United States, and upon the condition also that the said State of Texas shall by some solemn and authentic act of her Legislature or of a Convention, relinquish to the United States any claim which it has to any part of New Mexico.

"5th. Resolved that it is inexpedient to abolish Slavery in the District of Columbia, whilst that institution continues to exist, in the State of Maryland, without the consent of that State, without the consent of the people of the District, and without just compensation to the owners of slaves within the District.

"6th. But resolved that it is expedient to prohibit within the District the Slave trade in slaves brought into it from States or places beyond the limits of the District, either to be sold therein as merchandize or to be transported to other markets without the District of Columbia.

"7th. Resolved that more effectual provision ought to be made by law, according to the requirement of the Constitution, for the restitution and delivery of persons bound to service or labor in any State who may escape into any other State or Territory in the Union.

"And 8th. Resolved that Congress has no power to prohibit or obstruct the trade in Slaves between the Slaveholding States, but that the admission or exclusion of Slaves brought from one into another of them depends exclusively upon their own particular laws."

PRESIDENT MILLARD FILLMORE'S MESSAGE
TO THE HOUSE AND SENATE,
AUGUST 6, 1850, CONCERNING
THE TEXAS–NEW MEXICO BOUNDARY DISPUTE

This message decisively increased congressional support for passage of the Compromise of 1850. In it, President Millard Fillmore alerted Congress to the danger of a military confrontation between the United States and Texas over Santa Fe, emphatically rejected Texas's claim to all the lands east of the Rio Grande, urged Congress to draw a satisfactory boundary between New Mexico and Texas as quickly as possible, and indicated his support for passage of the remaining components of the compromise before Congress adjourned.

". . . Texas is a State, authorized to maintain her own laws so far as they are not repugnant to the Constitution, laws, and treaties of the United States; . . . But all this power is local and confined entirely within the limits of Texas herself. She can possibly confer no authority which can be lawfully exercised beyond her own boundaries.

"All this is plain, and hardly needs argument or elucidation. If Texas militia, therefore, march into any one of the other States or into any Territory of the United States, there to execute or enforce any law of Texas, they become at that moment trespassers; they are no longer under the protection of any lawful authority, and are to be regarded merely as intruders; and if within such State or Territory they obstruct any law of the United States, either by power of arms or mere power of numbers, constituting such a combination as is too powerful to be suppressed by the civil authority, the President of the United States has no option left to him, but is bound to obey the solemn injunction of the Constitution [to call up militia to suppress an insurrection] and exercise the high powers vested in him by that instrument and by the acts of Congress . . .

"The executive government of the United States has no power or authority to determine what was the true line of boundary between Mexico and the United States before the Treaty of Guadelupe Hidalgo, nor has it any such power now, since the question has become a question between the State of Texas and the United States. So far as this boundary is doubtful, that doubt can only be removed by some act of Congress, to which the assent of the State of Texas may be necessary, or by some appropriate mode of legal adjudication; but, in the meantime, if disturbances or collisions arise or should be threatened, it is absolutely incumbent on the executive government, however painful the duty, to take care that the laws shall be faithfully maintained; and he can regard only the actual state of things as existed at the date of the treaty . . . In other words, all must now be regarded as New Mexico which was possessed and occupied as New Mexico by citizens of Mexico at the date of the treaty until a definite line of boundary shall be established by competent authority . . .

"No government can be established for New Mexico, either State or Territorial, until it shall first be ascertained what New Mexico is, and what are her limits and boundaries. These can not be fixed or known till the line of division between her and Texas shall be ascertained and established; and numerous and weighty reasons conspire, in my judgment, to show that this divisional line should be established by Congress with the assent of the government of Texas. In the first place, this seems by far the most prompt mode of proceeding by which the end can be accomplished. If judicial proceedings were resorted to, such proceedings would necessarily be slow, and years would pass, in all probability, before the controversy could be ended. So great a delay in this case is to be avoided if possible. Such delay would be every way inconvenient, and might be the occasion of disturbances and collisions. For the same reason, I would with utmost deference to the wisdom of Congress, express a doubt of the expediency of the appointment of commissioners, and of an examination, estimate, and an award of indemnity to be made by them. This would be but a species of arbitration, which might last as long as a suit at law.

"So far as I am able to comprehend the case, the general facts are now all known, and Congress is as capable of deciding on it justly and properly now as it probably would be after the report of commissions. If the claim of title on the part of Texas appears to Congress to be well founded in whole or in part, it is in the competency of Congress to offer her an indemnity for the surrender of that claim. In a case like this, surrounded, as it is, by many cogent considerations, all calling for amicable adjustment and immediate settlement, the Government of the United States would be justified, in my opinion, in allowing an indemnity to Texas, not unreasonable or extravagant, but fair, liberal, and awarded in a just spirit of accommodation.

"I think no event would be hailed with more gratification by the people of the United States than the amicable adjustment of questions of difficulty which have now for a long time agitated the country and occupied, to the exclusion of other subjects, the time and attention of Congress.

"Having thus freely communicated the results of my own reflections on the most advisable mode of adjusting the boundary question, I shall nevertheless most cheerfully acquiesce in any other mode which the wisdom of Congress may devise. And in conclusion I repeat my conviction that every consideration of public interest manifests the necessity of a provision by Congress for the settlement of this boundary question before the present session be brought to a close. The settlement of other questions connected with the same subject within the same period is greatly to be desired, but the adjustment of this appears to me to be in the highest degree important."

APPEAL OF THE INDEPENDENT DEMOCRATS, JANUARY 1854

In response to the first two versions of Stephen A. Douglas's bill for organizing the Nebraska Territory, Massachusetts's Free-Soil Senator Charles Sumner, relying in part on a draft by Ohio's Free-Soil Congressman Joshua R. Giddings, penned this denunciation, which appeared in newspapers on January 24, 1854. By portraying the bill as a pro-slavery aggression by Southerners against the North, it preempted Douglas's planned justification of the measure as an embodiment of popular sovereignty and forced most southern Whigs in Congress to support the measure.

"As Senators and Representatives in the Congress of the United States it is our duty to warn our constituents, whenever imminent danger menaces the freedom of our institutions or the permanency of the Union.

"Such danger, as we firmly believe, now impends, and we earnestly solicit your prompt attention to it.

"At the last session of Congress a bill for the organization of the Territory of Nebraska passed the House of Representatives by an overwhelming majority. That bill was based on the principle of excluding slavery from the new Territory. It was not taken up for consideration in the Senate, and consequently failed to become a law.

"At the present session a new Nebraska Bill has been reported by the Senate Committee on Territories, which, should it unhappily receive the sanction of Congress, will open all the unorganized Territories of the Union to the ingress of slavery.

"We arraign this bill as a gross violation of a sacred pledge; as a criminal betrayal of precious rights; as part and parcel of an atrocious plot to exclude from a vast unoccupied region immigrants from the Old World and free laborers from our own States, and convert it into a dreary region of despotism, inhabited by masters and slaves . . .

"We beg your attention, fellow-citizens, to a few historical facts:

"The original settled policy of the United States, clearly indicated by the Jefferson proviso of 1784 and the Ordinance of 1787, was non-extension of slavery.

"In 1803, Louisiana was acquired by purchase from France. At that time there were some twenty-five or thirty thousand slaves in the Territory; most of them within what is now the State of Louisiana; a few only, farther north, on the west bank of the Mississippi. Congress, instead of providing for the abolition of slavery in this new Territory, permitted its continuance. In 1812 the State of Louisiana was organized and admitted into the Union with slavery.

"In 1818, six years later, the inhabitants of the Territory of Missouri applied to Congress for authority to form a State constitution, and for admission into the Union. There were, at that time, in the whole territory acquired from France, outside of the State of Louisiana, not three thousand slaves.

"There was no apology, in the circumstances of the country, for the continuance of slavery. The original national policy was against it, and not less the plain language of the treaty under which the territory had been acquired from France.

"It was proposed, therefore, to incorporate in the bill authorizing the formation of a State government, a provision requiring that the constitution of the new State should contain an article providing for the abolition of existing slavery, and prohibit the further introduction of slaves.

"This provision was vehemently and pertinaciously opposed, but finally prevailed in the House of Representatives by a decided vote. In the Senate it was rejected, and—in consequence of the disagreement between the two Houses—the bill was lost.

"At the next session of Congress, the controversy was renewed with increased violence. It was terminated at length by a compromise. Missouri was allowed to come into the Union with slavery; but a section was inserted in the act authorizing her admission, excluding slavery forever from all the territory acquired from France, not included in the new State, lying north of 36° 30'. We quote the prohibitory section:

"'Section 8. Be it further enacted, That in all that territory ceded by France to the United States, under the name of Louisiana, which lies north of 36° and 30' of north latitude, not included within the limits of the State contemplated by this act, slavery and involuntary servitude, otherwise than as the punishment of crimes, shall be and is hereby forever prohibited' . . .

"Nothing is more certain in history than the fact that Missouri could not have been admitted as a slave State had not certain members from the free States been reconciled to the measure by the incorporation of this prohibition into the act of admission. Nothing is more certain than that this prohibition has been regarded and accepted by the whole country as a solemn compact against the extension of slavery into any part of the territory acquired from France lying north of 36° 30', and not included in the new State of Missouri. The same act—let it be ever remembered—which authorized the formation of a constitution by the State, without a clause forbidding slavery, consecrated, beyond question and beyond honest recall, the whole remainder of the Territory to freedom and free institutions forever. For more than thirty years—during more than half our national existence under our present Constitution—this compact has been universally regarded and acted upon as inviolable American law. In conformity with it, Iowa was admitted as a free State and Minnesota has been organized as a free Territory.

"It is a strange and ominous fact, well calculated to awaken the worst apprehensions and the most fearful forebodings of future calamities, that it is now deliberately proposed to repeal this prohibition, by implication or directly—the latter certainly the manlier way—and thus to subvert the compact, and allow slavery in all the yet unorganized territory . . .

"In 1820 the slave States said to the free States: 'Admit Missouri with slavery, and refrain from positive exclusion south of 36° 30', and we will join you in perpetual prohibition north of that line.' The free States consented. In 1854 the slave States say to the free States: 'Missouri is admitted; no prohibition south of 36° 30' has been attempted; we have received the full consideration of our agreement; no more is to be gained by adherence to it on our part; we therefore propose to cancel the compact.' If this is not Punic faith, what is? Not without the deepest dishonor and crime can the free States acquiesce in the demand.

"We confess our total inability to delineate the character or describe the consequences of this measure. Language fails to express the sentiments of indignation and abhorrence which it inspires; and no vision less penetrating and comprehensive than that of the All-Seeing can reach its evil issues . . .

"We appeal to the people. We warn you that the dearest interests of freedom and the Union are in imminent peril. Demagogues may tell you that the Union can be maintained only by submitting to the demands of slavery. We tell you that the Union can only be maintained by the full recognition of the just claims of freedom and man. The Union was formed to establish justice and secure the blessings of liberty. When it fails to accomplish these ends it will be worthless, and when it becomes worthless it cannot long endure."

S. P. *Chase*, Senator from Ohio

Charles Sumner, Senator from Massachusetts

J. R. Giddings and *Edward Wade*, Representatives from Ohio

Gerrit Smith, Representative from New York

Alexander De Witt, Representative from Massachusetts

KANSAS-NEBRASKA ACT,
1854

Offered originally by Illinois's Democratic Senator Stephen A. Douglas as a bill to organize a single Nebraska territory, this bill was amended in response to pressure from some northern and most southern Democrats into a form that effectively repealed the Missouri Compromise's prohibition of slavery extension. The final act outraged most Northerners and helped revolutionize political alignments in the North. Printed below are the two sections of the final act that substituted popular sovereignty in the new territories for the 1820 language that "forever prohibited" slavery from them.

"Section 14. That the Constitution, and all the laws of the United States which are not locally inapplicable, shall have the same force and effect within the Territory of Nebraska as elsewhere within the United States, except the eighth section of the act preparatory to the admission of Missouri into the Union . . .

which, being inconsistent with the principle of non-intervention by Congress with slavery in the States and Territories, as recognized by the legislation of eighteen hundred and fifty, commonly called the compromise measures, is hereby declared inoperative and void; it being the true intent and meaning of this act not to legislate slavery into any Territory or State, nor exclude it therefrom, but to leave the people thereof perfectly free to form and regulate their domestic institutions in their own way, subject only to the Constitution of the United States: *Provided*, That nothing herein contained shall be construed to revive or put force into any law or regulation which may have existed prior to the act of sixth March, eighteen hundred and twenty, either protecting, establishing, prohibiting, or abolishing slavery."

"Section 19. . . . and when admitted as a State or States, the said Territory, or any portion of the same, shall be received into the Union with or without slavery, as their constitution may prescribe at the time of their admission."

ABRAHAM LINCOLN'S "HOUSE DIVIDED" SPEECH, JUNE 16, 1858

After Illinois's Democratic Senator Stephen A. Douglas joined Republicans in Congress in attempting to block Kansas's admission as a slave state under the Lecompton Constitution, many eastern Republicans pressured Illinois Republicans to allow Douglas's reelection to the Senate in 1858. Instead, Illinois Republicans at their June 1858 state convention nominated Abraham Lincoln as their candidate for the Senate, should Republicans win the November legislative elections. In this speech accepting that nomination, Lincoln attempted to define the differences between Republicans and Democrats on slavery extension and to arraign Democratic legislation for allowing it. Lincoln adumbrated these themes in his famous debates with Douglas later that summer, where, even more than here, he stressed the immorality of slavery as the primary reason for opposing its extension. To justify Republicans' opposition to Douglas, Lincoln here also raises the specter of a Democratic plot to obtain another Supreme Court decision extending slavery to the existing free states, not just to western territories.

"If we could first know *where* we are, and *whither* we are tending, we could then better judge *what* to do, and *how* to do it.

"We are now into the *fifth* year, since a policy was initiated, with the *avowed* object, and *confident* promise, of putting an end to slavery agitation.

"Under the operation of that policy, that agitation has not only, *not ceased*, but has *constantly augmented*.

"In my opinion, it *will* not cease, until a *crisis* shall have been reached, and passed.

"'A house divided against itself cannot stand.'

"I believe this government cannot endure, permanently half *slave* and half *free*.

"I do not expect the Union to be *dissolved*—I do not expect the house to *fall*—but I *do* expect it will cease to be divided.

"It will become *all* one thing, or *all* the other.

"Either the *opponents* of slavery, will arrest the further spread of it, and place it where the public mind shall rest in the belief that it is in course of ultimate extinction; or its *advocates* will push it forward, till it shall become alike lawful in *all* the States, *old* as well as *new*—*North* as well as *South*.

"Have we no *tendency* to the latter condition?

"Let anyone who doubts, carefully contemplate that now

almost complete legal combination—piece of *machinery* so to speak—compounded of the Nebraska doctrine, and the Dred Scott decision. Let him consider not only *what work* the machinery is adapted to do, and *how well* adapted; but also, let him study the *history* of its construction, and trace, if he can, or rather *fail*, if he can, to trace the evidences of design, and concert of action, among its chief bosses, from the beginning . . .

"We cannot absolutely *know* that all these exact adaptations are the result of preconcert. But when we see a lot of framed timbers, different portions of which we know have been gotten out at different times and places and by different workmen— Stephen [Douglas], Franklin [Pierce], Roger [Taney] and James [Buchanan], for instance—and when we see these timbers joined together, and see they exactly make the frame of a house or a mill, all the tenons and mortices exactly fitting, and all the lengths and proportions of the different pieces exactly adapted to their respective places, and not a piece too many or too few— not omitting even scaffolding—or, if a single piece be lacking, we can see the place in the frame exactly fitted and prepared to yet bring such piece in—in *such* a case, we find it impossible to not *believe* that Stephen and Franklin and Roger and James all understood one another from the beginning, and all worked upon a common *plan* or *draft* drawn up before the first lick was struck . . .

". . . Put *that* and *that* together, and we have another nice little niche, which we may, ere long, see filled with another Supreme Court decision, declaring that the Constitution of the United States does not permit a *state* to exclude slavery from its limits.

"And this may especially be expected if the doctrine of 'care not whether slavery be voted *down* or voted *up*,' shall gain upon the public mind sufficiently to give promise that such a decision can be maintained when made.

"Such a decision is all that slavery now lacks of being alike lawful in all the States.

"Welcome or unwelcome, such decision *is* probably coming, and will soon be upon us, unless the power of the present political dynasty shall be met and overthrown.

"We shall *lie down* pleasantly dreaming that the people of *Missouri* are on the verge of making their State *free*; and we shall awake to the *reality*, instead, that the Supreme Court has made *Illinois* a *slave* State.

"To meet and overthrow the power of that dynasty, is the work now before all those who would prevent that consummation.

"That is *what* we have to do.

"But *how* can we best do it?

"There are those who denounce us *openly* to their *own* friends, and yet whisper *us softly*, that *Senator Douglas* is the *aptest* instrument there is, with which to effect that object. *They* do *not* tell us, nor has *he* told us, that he *wishes* any such object to be effected. They wish us to *infer* all, from the facts, that he now has a little quarrel with the present head of the dynasty; and that he has regularly voted with us, on a single point, upon which, he and we, have never differed.

"They remind us that *he* is a very *great man*, and that the largest of *us* are very small ones. Let this be granted. But 'a *living dog* is better than a *dead lion*.' Judge Douglas, if not a *dead* lion *for this work*, is at least a *caged* and *toothless* one. How can he oppose the advances of slavery? He don't *care* anything about it. His avowed *mission is impressing* the 'public heart' to *care* nothing about it.

"A leading Douglas Democratic newspaper thinks Douglas' superior talent will be needed to resist the revival of the African slave trade.

"Does Douglas believe an effort to revive that trade is approaching? He has not said so. Does he *really* think so? But if it is, how can he resist it? For years he has labored to prove it a *sacred right* of white men to take negro slaves into the new territories. Can he possibly show that it is *less* a sacred right to *buy* them where they can be bought cheapest? And, unquestionably they can be bought *cheaper in Africa* than in *Virginia.*

"He has recently done all in his power to reduce the whole question of slavery to one of a mere *right of property*; and as such, how can *he* oppose the foreign slave trade—how can he refuse that trade in that 'property' shall be 'perfectly free'—unless he does it as a *protection* to the home production? And as the home *producers* will probably not *ask* the protection, he will be wholly without a ground of opposition.

"Senator Douglas holds, we know, that a man may rightfully be *wiser to-day* than he was *yesterday*—that he may rightfully *change* when he finds himself wrong.

"But, can we for that reason, run ahead, and *infer* that he *will* make any particular change, of which he, himself, has given no intimation? Can we *safely* base *our* action upon any such *vague* inference?

"Now, as ever, I wish not to *misrepresent* Judge Douglas' *position*, question his *motives*, or do ought that can be personally offensive to him.

"Whenever, *if ever*, he and we can come together on *principle* so that *our great cause* may have assistance from *his great ability*, I hope to have imposed no adventitious obstacle.

"But clearly, he is not *now* with us—he does not pretend to be—he does not *promise* to *ever* be.

"Our cause, then, must be intrusted to and conducted by its own undoubted friends—those whose hands are free, whose hearts are in the work—who *do care* for the result.

"Two years ago the Republicans of the nation mustered over thirteen hundred thousand strong.

"We did this under the single impulse of resistance to a common danger, with every external circumstance against us.

"Of *strange, discordant,* and even, *hostile* elements, we gathered from the four winds, and *formed* and fought the battle through, under the constant hot fire of a disciplined, proud, and pampered enemy.

"Did we brave all *then,* to *falter* now?—*now*—when that same enemy is *wavering,* dissevered and belligerent?

"The result is not doubtful. We shall not fail—if we stand firm, we shall not fail.

"*Wise councils* may *accelerate* or *mistakes delay* it, but, sooner or later that victory is *sure* to come."

WILLIAM H. SEWARD'S "IRREPRESSIBLE CONFLICT" SPEECH, ROCHESTER, NEW YORK, OCTOBER 25, 1858

In 1858 New York's Senator William H. Seward was by far the most prominent Republican politician in the nation. Here, like Lincoln in Illinois, he tried to justify the continuing existence of the Republican Party now that slavery's possible extension to Kansas appeared to have been stopped. Where Lincoln pointed to the threat of a new Supreme Court decision legalizing slavery throughout the North as the rationale for continued Republican opposition to Democrats, however, Seward postulated that political conflict between profoundly different northern and southern social orders was inevitable and explicitly identified the Democratic Party as the agent of Slave Power aggressions against the North, thus requiring a northern champion, the Republican Party, to oust it from power.

This famous speech influenced numerous historians' interpretation of the causes of the Civil War for many generations, but it also illustrates marvelously the dynamics of partisan electoral conflict in the antebellum period. Each party defined its differences from the opponent as starkly as possible, and then flailed the many real and purported failings of that opponent. No one then believed that "moving to the center" was the way to win elections.

"Fellow-Citizens: The unmistakable outbreaks of zeal which occur all around me, show that you are earnest men—and such a man am I. Let us, therefore, at least for a time, pass by all secondary and collateral questions, whether of a personal or of a general nature, and consider the main subject of the present canvass [the congressional and state elections of 1858]. The Democratic party, or, to speak more accurately, the party which wears that attractive name, is in possession of the Federal Government. The Republicans propose to dislodge that party, and dismiss it from its high trust.

"The main subject, then, is, whether the Democratic party deserves to retain the confidence of the American people. In attempting to prove it unworthy, I think that I am not actuated by prejudices against that party, or by prepossessions in favor of its adversary; for I have learned, by some experience, that virtue and patriotism, vice and selfishness, are found in all parties, and that they differ less in their motives than in the policies they pursue.

"Our country is a theatre, which exhibits in full operation, two radically different political systems; the one resting on the basis of servile or slave labor, the other on the voluntary labor of freemen.

"The laborers who are enslaved are all negroes, or persons more or less purely of African derivation. But this is only accidental. The principle of the system is, that labor in every society, by whomsoever performed, is necessarily unintellectual, groveling, and base; and that the laborer, equally for his own good and for the welfare of the State, ought to be enslaved. The white laboring man, whether native or foreigner, is not enslaved, only because he cannot, as yet, be reduced to bondage . . .

"The slave system is one of constant danger, distrust, suspicion, and watchfulness. It debases those whose toil alone can produce wealth and resources for defense, to the lowest degree of which human nature is capable, to guard against mutiny and insurrection, and thus wastes energies which otherwise might be employed in national development and aggrandizement.

"The free-labor system educates all alike, and by opening all the fields of industrial employment, and all the departments of authority, to the unchecked and equal rivalry of all classes of men, at once secures universal contentment, and brings into the highest possible activity all the physical, moral, and social energies of the whole State. In States where the slave system prevails, the masters, directly or indirectly, secure all political power, and constitute a ruling aristocracy. In States where the free-labor system prevails, universal suffrage necessarily obtains, and the State inevitably becomes, sooner or later, a republic or democracy . . .

"Hitherto, the two systems have existed in different States, but side by side within the American Union. This has happened because the Union is a confederation of States. But in another aspect the United States constitute only one nation. Increase of population, which is filling the States out to their very borders, together with a new and extended net-work of railroads and other avenues, and an internal commerce which daily becomes more intimate, is rapidly bringing the States into a higher and more perfect social unity or consolidation. Thus, these antagonistic systems are continually coming into closer contact, and collision results.

"Shall I tell you what this collision means? They who think that it is accidental, unnecessary, the work of interested or fanatical agitators, and therefore ephemeral, mistake the case altogether. It is an irrepressible conflict between opposing and enduring forces, and it means that the United States must and will, sooner or later, become either entirely a slaveholding nation, or entirely a free-labor nation. Either the cotton and rice fields of South Carolina and the sugar plantations of Louisiana will ultimately be filled by free labor, and Charleston and New Orleans become marts for legitimate merchandise alone, or else the rye-fields and wheat-fields of Massachusetts and New-York must again be surrendered by their farmers to slave culture and to the production of slaves, and Boston and New-York become once more markets for trade in the bodies and souls of men. It is the failure to apprehend this great truth that induces so many unsuccessful attempts at final compromise between the Slave and Free States, and it is the existence of this great fact that renders all such pretended compromises, when made, vain and ephemeral . . .

". . . In the field of federal politics, Slavery, deriving unlooked-for advantages from commercial changes, and energies unforeseen from the facilities of combination between members of the slaveholding class and between that class and other property classes, early rallied, and has at length made a stand, not merely to retain its original defensive position, but to extend its sway throughout the whole Union. It is certain that the slaveholding class of American citizens indulge this high ambition, and that they derive encouragement for it from the rapid and effective political successes which they have already obtained. The plan of operation is this: By continued appliances of patronage and threats of disunion, they will keep a majority favorable to these designs in the Senate, where each State has an equal representation. Through that majority they will defeat, as they best can, the admission of Free States, and secure the admission of Slave States. Under the protection of the Judiciary, they will, on the principle of the Dred Scott case, carry Slavery into all the Territories of the United States now existing, and hereafter to be organized. By the action of the President and the Senate, using the treaty-making power, they will annex foreign slaveholding States. In a favorable conjuncture they will induce Congress to repeal the act of 1808, which prohibits the foreign slave-trade, and so they will import from Africa, at the cost of only $20 a head, slaves enough to fill up the interior of the continent. Thus relatively increasing the number of Slave States, they will allow no amendment to the Constitution prejudicial to their interest; and so, having permanently established their power, they expect the Federal Judiciary to nullify all State laws which shall interfere with internal or foreign commerce in slaves. When the Free States shall be sufficiently demoralized to tolerate these designs, they reasonably conclude that Slavery will be accepted by those States themselves . . .

"The very constitution of the Democratic party commits it to execute all the designs of the slaveholders, whatever they may be. It is not a party of the whole Union, of all the Free States and of all the Slave States; nor yet is it a party of the Free States in the North and in the Northwest; but it is a sectional and local party, having practically its seat within the Slave States, and counting its constituency chiefly and almost exclusively there. Of all its representatives in Congress and in the Electoral College, two-thirds uniformly come from these States. Its great element of strength lies in the vote of the slaveholders, augmented by the representation of three-fifths of the slaves. Deprive the Democratic party of this strength, and it would be a helpless and hopeless minority, incapable of continued organization. The

Democratic party, being thus local and sectional, acquires new strength from the admission of every new Slave State, and loses relatively by the admission of every new Free State into the Union . . .

"To expect the Democratic party to resist Slavery and favor Freedom, is as unreasonable as to look for Protestant missionaries to the Catholic Propaganda of Rome. The history of the Democratic party commits it to the policy of Slavery. It has been the Democratic party, and no other agency, which has carried that policy up to its present alarming culmination . . .

". . . I know—few, I think, know better than I—the resources and energies of the Democratic party, which is identical with the Slave Power . . . The Democratic party derived its strength, originally, from its adoption of the principles of equal and exact justice to all men. So long as it practiced this principle faithfully, it was invulnerable. It became vulnerable when it renounced the principle, and since that time it has maintained itself, not by virtue of its own strength, or even of its traditional merits, but because there as yet had appeared in the political field no other party that had the conscience and the courage to take up, and avow, and practice the life-inspiring principles which the Democratic party had surrendered. At last, the Republican party has appeared. It avows now, as the Republican party of 1800 did, in one word, its faith and its works, 'Equal and exact justice to all men.' Even when it first entered the field, only half organized, it struck a blow which only just failed to secure complete and triumphant victory. In this, its second campaign, it has already won advantages which render that triumph now both easy and certain.

"The secret of its assured success lies in the very characteristic which, in the mouth of scoffers, constitutes its great and lasting imbecility and reproach. It lies in the fact that it is a party of one idea; but that idea is a noble one—an idea that fills and expands all generous souls; the idea of equality—the equality of all men before human tribunals and human laws, as they all are equal before the Divine tribunal and Divine laws."

SUGGESTIONS FOR FURTHER READING

The literature on the causes of the Civil War and the slavery extension issue from 1820 to 1861 is enormous, and this note makes no attempt to be comprehensive. Rather, it is confined to a relatively brief list of books and articles most relevant to the subject matter of this book.

Two superb books treat the events covered here comprehensively: David M. Potter, *The Impending Crisis, 1848–1861*, completed and edited by Don E. Fehrenbacher (New York: Harper and Row, 1976); and William W. Freehling, *The Road to Disunion, Volume I: Secessionists at Bay, 1776–1854* (New York: Oxford University Press, 1990). In *The South and the Politics of Slavery, 1828–1856* (Baton Rouge: Louisiana State University Press, 1978), William J. Cooper Jr. assesses the role of slavery in antebellum southern politics in a way different from Freehling. The interpretation advanced here differs in some respects from these books, and I have presented it with more detailed evidence in two previous books, although each of those books had a different focus from this one: Michael F. Holt, *The Political Crisis of the 1850s* (repr. ed., New York: W. W. Norton and Company, 1983); and Michael F. Holt, *The Rise and Fall of the American Whig Party: Jacksonian Politics and the Onset of the Civil War* (New York: Oxford University Press, 1999). The slavery extension issue and its political ramifications throughout the four decades prior to the Civil War are treated in considerable detail and with astute analysis in Michael A. Morrison, *Slavery and the American West: The Eclipse of Manifest Destiny and the Coming of the Civil War* (Chapel Hill: University of North Carolina Press, 1997).

Glover B. Moore, *The Missouri Controversy, 1819–1821* (Lexington: University of Kentucky Press, 1953), is the standard monograph on the Missouri Compromise, but it is now dated and should be supplemented with Freehling's book and Don E. Fehrenbacher, *The South and Three Sectional Crises* (Baton Rouge: Louisiana State University Press, 1980).

The best study of James K. Polk's expansionist vision and the first two years of his administration remains Charles G. Sellers Jr., *James K. Polk, Continentalist, 1843–1846* (Princeton, N.J.: Princeton University Press, 1966), but see also David M. Pletcher, *The Diplomacy of Annexation: Texas, Oregon, and the Mexican War* (Columbia: University of Missouri Press, 1973), and Paul H. Bergeron, *The Presidency of James K. Polk* (Lawrence: University Press of Kansas, 1987).

The standard monograph on the introduction of the Wilmot Proviso is Chaplain W. Morrison, *Democratic Politics and Sectionalism: The Wilmot Proviso Controversy* (Chapel Hill: University of North Carolina Press, 1967). It should be supplemented, however, with Eric Foner, "The Wilmot Proviso Revisited," *Journal of American History* 56 (1969), pp. 262–79, a seminal article on which I have relied heavily for quotations in the text.

The presidential election of 1848 is treated at greater length in Freehling's *Road to Disunion* and my two previous books mentioned above, but see also Joseph G. Rayback, *Free Soil: The Election of 1848* (Lexington: University Press of Kentucky, 1970). For more on the Free-Soil Party, see Frederick J. Blue, *The Free Soilers: Third Party Politics, 1848–1854* (Urbana: University of Illinois Press, 1973), and Richard H. Sewell, *Ballots for Freedom: Antislavery Politics in the United States, 1837–1860* (New York: Oxford University Press, 1976).

My *Rise and Fall of the American Whig Party* contains the most recent, detailed analysis of Zachary Taylor's presidency, but see also Holman Hamilton, *Zachary Taylor: Soldier in the White House* (repr. ed., Hamden, Conn.: Archon Books, 1966), and Elbert B. Smith, *The Presidencies of Zachary Taylor and Millard Fillmore* (Lawrence: University Press of Kansas, 1988). For years the standard monograph on the Compromise of 1850 was Holman Hamilton, *Prologue to Conflict: The Crisis and Compromise of 1850* (New York: W. W. Norton and Company, 1964), but it has recently been importantly supplemented, if not supplanted, by Mark J. Stegmaier, *Texas, New Mexico, and the Compromise of 1850: Boundary Dispute & Sectional Crisis* (Kent, Ohio: Kent State University Press, 1996), a marvelous piece of scholarship that demonstrates beyond cavil that the boundary dispute was at the heart of congressional debates in 1850.

For the complex motives behind the framing of the Kansas-Nebraska Act in 1854, I have relied heavily on Roy Franklin Nichols, "The Kansas-Nebraska Act: A Century of Historiography," *Mississippi Valley Historical Review* 43 (1956), pp. 187–212. Significant variations on Nichols's interpretation are in Robert W. Johannsen, *Stephen A. Douglas* (New York: Oxford University Press, 1973), and Freehling, *Road to Disunion*.

I have treated the disruption and disintegration of the Whig Party between 1854 and 1857 in considerable detail in my *Rise and Fall of the American Whig Party*. Absolutely the best study of the emergence of the Republican Party during those years, its relationship with Know-Nothingism, and the election of 1856 is William E. Gienapp, *The Origins of the Republican Party, 1852–1856* (New York: Oxford University Press, 1987). The now-standard analysis of the reasons for the early Republican Party's steadfast commitment against slavery extension, however, is Eric Foner, *Free Soil, Free Labor, Free Men: The Ideology of the Republican Party before the Civil War* (New York: Oxford University Press, 1970). Readers should be aware, however, that Freehling, Gienapp, and I dissent somewhat from Foner's assertion that a "free labor" ideal lay at the core of Republicans' opposition to slavery extension.

Don E. Fehrenbacher's Pulitzer Prize–winning *The Dred Scott Case: Its Significance in American Law and Politics* (New York: Oxford University Press, 1978) not only presents the finest analysis of that controversial decision ever written, it also provides a splendid overview of the slavery extension issue since the nation's founding and of Congress's contested constitutional authority to bar slavery from territories. The best analysis of the divisive impact of disputes over Kansas's Lecompton Constitution on the Democratic Party remains Roy Franklin Nichols, *Disruption of American Democracy* (New York: Macmillan, 1948), but for that impact and events in Kansas see also James A. Rawley, *Race and Politics: "Bleeding Kansas" and the Coming of the Civil War* (Philadelphia: J. B. Lippincott, 1969), and Kenneth M. Stampp, *America in 1857: A Nation on the Brink* (New York: Oxford University Press, 1990). The literature on the Lincoln-Douglas debates of 1858 is itself enormous. The most astute analyses of them, however, remain Harry V. Jaffa, *Crisis of the House Divided: An Interpretation of the Issues in the Lincoln-Douglas Debates* (Garden City, N.Y.: Doubleday, 1959), Don E. Fehrenbacher, *Prelude to Greatness: Lincoln in the 1850s* (Stanford, Calif.: Stanford University Press, 1962), and David Herbert Donald, *Lincoln* (New York: Simon and Schuster, 1995).

I have made no attempt in this little book to account for southern secession in response to Lincoln's election or Republicans' reaction to it in the winter of 1860–61. For the latter matter, however, see David M. Potter, *Lincoln and His Party in the Secession Crisis* (New Haven, Conn.: Yale University Press, 1942), Kenneth M. Stampp, *And the War Came: The North and the Secession Crisis, 1860–61* (Baton Rouge: Louisiana State University Press, 1950), and especially Daniel W. Crofts, *Reluctant Confederates: Upper South Unionists in the Secession Crisis* (Chapel Hill: University of North Carolina Press, 1989).

INDEX

abolition, 4–6, 54, 61, 107, 141–42;
English advocacy of, 10; Lincoln's
position on, 112; in Mexico, 37,
46, 53, 66, 69–71
abolitionists, 107, 116–17
Adams, Charles Francis, 44
Adams, John Quincy, 8
Alabama, 36, 101; secessionists in, 83;
Union Party in, 84
Allen, William, 63
American Party, see Know-Nothing
Party
Anglo-American Convention (1818),
24, 25
Arkansas, admission to Union of, 93
Atchison, David R., 94, 99, 100, 116

Bank of the United States, 8
Barnburners, 62, 97–98, 102, 104
Bell, John, 106, 108
Bell, Peter H., 75–76, 78
Benton, Thomas Hart, 11, 14, 46,
73, 94
Berrien, John M., 33, 37

blacks, free, 27, 116
"Bleeding Kansas," 117, 118, 120
Border Ruffians, 116, 117, 120
Breckinridge, John C., 122
Bright, Jesse D., 62
Brooks, Preston S., 118
Brown, John, 117
Brown, Milton, 13–15, 38, 103
Buchanan, James, 125, 147; and
admission of Kansas to Union,
120, 121; presidential candidacy
of, 35, 37, 110, 118, 123
Buena Vista, battle of, 40
Butler, Andrew Pickens, 99, 117–18

Calhoun, John C., 25, 31, 33–36,
73, 99; Southern Address of, 53–
54, 58, 94
California, 16, 18, 45, 93, 95, 132;
and Compromise of 1850, 69,
70, 72–74, 79, 81, 135; gold rush
in, 50–51, 89; Polk's map of,
51–52; Preston's statehood bill for,
55–56, 64; proposed extension of